While every precaution has been taken in the preparation of this book, the publisher assumes no responsibility for errors or omissions, or for damages resulting from the use of the information contained herein.

QUANTUM QUANDARIES

First edition. August 8, 2023.

Copyright © 2023 Lab Maharaj.

ISBN: 979-8223447405

Written by Lab Maharaj.

I am humbled and honoured to express my deepest gratitude and dedicate it to all those who have inspired me on this incredible journey. First and foremost, I would like to dedicate this book to my best friend Adam, whose unwavering support and profound insights have propelled me towards a deeper understanding of the universe. Adam's contagious enthusiasm for science ignited a fire within me, leading me on a quest for knowledge that has shaped every word written here.

Furthermore, I extend my heartfelt dedication to the countless individuals whose contributions have influenced my writing. From esteemed scientists who paved the way with groundbreaking discoveries to philosophers who meditated upon the mysteries of existence, their brilliance has been an unceasing source of inspiration.

Quantum Quandaries: Navigating the Intersection of Computing and Physics

By Lab Maharaj

I

Introduction

Computing and physics are two distinct yet highly interconnected domains of science. Computing, essentially a data manipulation science, heavily pivots on the principles of mathematics, logical reasoning, and algorithmic foundations. Physics, on the other hand, explores the fundamental properties and nature of the universe, chiefly harnessing the principles of space, time, matter, and energy.

Introducing the Intersection of Computing and Physics

The intersection of computing and physics has proven demanding, swelling the need to comprehend their inevitable and instrumental correlation. The advancing technological landscape has seen a heightened merger of physics and computing, shaping a profound domain known as computational physics. Computational physics is an important subset bridging the divide between physics and computer science, leveraging computational algorithms and numerical analysis to solve and visualise complex physics problems. The need to solve intricate problems across various physics realms, from fluid dynamics, quantum mechanics to astrological calculations, has fuelled the fusion of computing and physics for advanced research and application.

The history of overlapping physics and computing dates back to the 17th century when Sir Isaac Newton leveraged numerical methods to solve physics models, cementing a fundamental relationship between the two disciplines. But arguably, the true intersection of physics and computing began with the development of computing machines in the mid-20th century, innovatively harnessed for computing vast and convoluted physics calculations. Pioneering works from John von Neumann, Enrico Fermi, and others highlight the origin of computational physics, forever binding these disciplines together.

In more recent times, the evolution of quantum mechanics has significantly impacted the computing field, birthing quantum computing. Quantum computing harnesses quantum bits or 'qubits,' facilitating exponentially more processing power than traditional binary-based computing. Quantum computing, inspired and rooted in quantum mechanics principles, offers enormous potential to transform the computational world, further interweaving the threads of physics and computing.

The incredibly precise field of physics requires an equally meticulous numerical handling of operations like differential equations and integrations, where computing science comes into play. From programming languages like FORTRAN to Python, physicists have utilised them to represent and solve their complex models digitally. Algorithms, a fundamental of computing science, are heavily utilised in computational physics, allowing for the robust and systematic solution of vast arrays of physics problems.

Interestingly, advancements in machine learning and artificial intelligence, branches of computer science, are now being utilised in physics research. For example, machine learning algorithms have emerged as an invaluable watchdog in the Large Hadron Collider, warning scientists of any anomalies that could damage this expensive equipment. The influence computing has on physics and vice versa is monumental. Without the frameworks laid down by physics, the operation of many computing elements would be near impossible. Likewise, without computing, the modelling, calculation, and visualisation of physics data would be exceedingly challenging.

Analysing Data and Theories at the Intersection

The synthesis of computing and physics has opened up a novel avenue of scientific exploration characterised by the analysis of massive datasets and the application of powerful algorithms. This interdisciplinary approach has enabled researchers to uncover previously inaccessible patterns, detect anomalies, and better understand the universe. High-performance computing systems have enabled scientists to process and analyse data more rapidly than ever before, providing a platform to test existing theories against empirical evidence on an unprecedented scale.

With the help of advanced algorithms and machine learning techniques, vast amounts of experimental observations can be processed, revealing hidden patterns or unexpected correlations that may have previously gone unnoticed. Moreover, these powerful analytical tools enable researchers to validate or refine existing theories by comparing their predictions with experimental results on an unprecedented scale. In subsequent chapters, we will delve into various data analysis techniques employed by physicists, ranging from statistical methods to machine learning algorithms.

An Overview of the Topics that will be addressed:

Large Scale Experiments and Big Data

Handling

High energy physics, astronomy, and cosmology are notable areas of physics that rely heavily on sophisticated computing technologies for data processing and analysis. Here, experiments often generate enormous amounts of data, in the petabyte-scale and beyond. The Large Hadron Collider (LHC) at CERN, for example, generates more than one petabyte of data every second. This unprecedented volume of data necessitates efficient algorithms and high-performance computing platforms for data storage, processing, and analysis.

Data analysis tools allow the extraction of meaningful, tangible information from the seemingly impenetrable mass of raw data generated. Machine learning (ML) and artificial intelligence (AI) technologies, rooted in computer science, come in handy for pattern recognition, anomaly detection, and data modelling in these high-dimensional datasets, transforming the paradigm of data-driven physics research.

Ground breaking Discoveries

The intersection of computing and physics has directly contributed to remarkable advancements and breakthroughs. For instance, the detection of the Higgs boson and gravitational waves were facilitated through complex calculus and simulations run on high-performance computing systems. These pioneering discoveries highlight the priceless role of computing in the process of shaping physical theories and testing them, marking a paradigm shift in experimental physics. Such examples underscore the interconnectedness of both disciplines and illuminate the potential of their intersection.

Theoretical Modelling and Computation

Conceptually underpinning physical phenomena is an arduous task requiring stellar computational strength. Mainly because the behaviours of aggregated systems, like clusters of galaxies or even complex quantum systems, can be phenomenally intricate. High-performance computers and intricate numerical algorithms are applied in solving such probative complexities.

Theoretical physics, subatomic particles, relativistic quantum mechanics, particle interactions, cosmological phenomena, and even climate modelling involve complex modelling, entailing substantial computation. Sophisticated data visualisation tools further allow scientists to represent and intuitively understand such complex phenomena.

Embracing the empirical realities, physics is increasingly becoming computation-intensive. Integrative effort at the intersection of physics and computing indeed promises revelations about the universe, the vast cosmos, and even the tiny quantum worlds.

This intersection of computing and physics seamlessly merging data analysis and theories is a giant leap forward, facilitating scientific exploration and reverence toward the hidden marvels of our profound universe.

Role of computing in physics research

The advent of computing has revolutionised the landscape of physics research, rendering it an indispensable tool for scientists in their pursuit of understanding the fundamental laws governing our universe. The interplay between physics and computing has emerged as a symbiotic relationship, wherein computational techniques provide novel avenues to tackle complex scientific problems, while also facilitating deeper insights into the theoretical foundations of the discipline.

In the realm of physics research, computing enables researchers to simulate intricate physical phenomena that would otherwise be challenging or impossible to study directly through experimental means. Utilising computational models and algorithms, scientists can explore a wide range of scenarios and variables, allowing them to investigate intricate systems such as quantum mechanics, astrophysical phenomena, or fluid dynamics. Through computation-driven simulations and numerical analyses, physicists are able to gain valuable insights into the behaviour and properties of these systems, thereby unlocking new frontiers in scientific inquiry.

Furthermore, computing plays a vital role in theoretical physics by assisting scientists in formulating and solving complex mathematical equations that underpin various physical theories. As modern physics delves into increasingly abstract realms at the microcosmic level or explores uncharted territories like string theory or cosmology, sophisticated computational methods become crucial in establishing mathematical frameworks for these theories. By employing advanced algorithms and high-performance computing architectures, physicists can explore intricate mathematical models with greater accuracy and efficiency, ultimately enriching our understanding of fundamental phenomena.

One key area we shall address is the utilisation of high-performance computing (HPC) infrastructure for simulating intricate physical processes. This entails harnessing parallel computing paradigms, exploiting parallelism across multiple cores or distributed platforms, to expedite simulations that would otherwise be computationally prohibitive. Additionally, we shall investigate novel approaches like quantum computing that promise unprecedented computational prowess for tackling problems involving quantum mechanics and condensed matter physics.

The book will explore the realm of data-driven physics research by leveraging techniques from machine learning and artificial intelligence. The amalgamation of these powerful methodologies with traditional physics models holds immense potential for uncovering hidden patterns and correlations within experimental data. Such data-centric approaches enable us to extract valuable insights from vast datasets, leading to breakthroughs in fields ranging from cosmology and astrophysics to particle physics and quantum optics.

II

Exploring the Laws of Physics

At its core, the Laws of Physics embody a comprehensive framework that allows us to describe and predict the natural phenomena surrounding us. These laws are not arbitrary impositions but rather elegant expressions of observed regularities that have withstood intense scrutiny and empirical testing. From Newton's laws of motion to Maxwell's equations governing electromagnetism, each law stands as a pillar upon which our scientific edifice is constructed.

Foundations of Classical Mechanics

Classical mechanics is a fundamental branch of physics that deals with the motion of objects and the forces acting upon them. It lays down the basic principles that govern the movement of everything from tiny particles to celestial bodies. The foundations of classical mechanics were first established by Sir Isaac Newton in his ground breaking work, "Mathematical Principles of Natural Philosophy," published in 1687.

Newton's Laws of Motion

Newton's Laws of Motion, encapsulating Sir Isaac Newton's seminal contributions to classical mechanics, represent a foundational pillar of physical understanding in the academic realm. Sporting an unwavering intellectual rigour and an elegant mathematical formulation, these laws elucidate the fundamental principles governing the motion of objects in our tangible universe.

Law I: The Law of Inertia

Newton's first law, commonly known as the law of inertia, states that an object either remains at rest or continues to move at a constant velocity unless acted upon by an external force. In mathematical terms, Newton's first law can be written as $F = 0$ when $a = 0$, where 'F' represents force, and 'a' represents acceleration. The law implies that objects resist changes in their state of motion, a property known as inertia.

Law II: Law of Acceleration

Newton's second law, F = ma, describes the relationship between an object's mass, its acceleration, and the amount of force it experiences. The law states that the force exerted on an object is equal to the mass of the object multiplied by its acceleration. Therefore, an object's acceleration is directly proportional to the net force and inversely proportional to its mass. This law is foundational for studying flight dynamics, fluid mechanics, and numerous engineering applications.

Law III: Action and Reaction

Newton's third law, commonly known as the law of action and reaction, states that for every action, there is an equal and opposite reaction. This means that any force exerted on a body will create a force of equal magnitude but in the opposite direction on the object that exerted the first force. Mathematically, this law can be written as F12 = - F21, where F12 is the force exerted by body 1 on body 2, and F21 is the force exposed by body 2 on body 1. This law is vital in areas like rocket propulsion.

Implications of Newton's Laws

The laws have immense value across an array of disciplines. They form the foundation for the principles of conservation of momentum and angular momentum, crucial in both classical and quantum physics. Moreover, understanding these laws is prerequisite for navigating the realm of mechanical systems and other foundational engineering concepts. Despite their initial formulation centuries ago, Newton's laws continue to be instrumental in our daily lives, from pushing a shopping cart to launching spacecraft.

Conservation of Momentum

The Conservation of Momentum can be understood as an attribute of a system where the total momentum remains unvarying unless acted upon by external forces. The total momentum of a closed system, a system that does not interact with an external force, remains constant irrespective of the internal actions within the system. Therefore, when two bodies interact in a closed system, the total momentum before interaction will be equal to the total momentum after the interaction, considering no external forces have acted upon it in the meantime.

This principle manifests in various everyday occurrences, from the simplest action of pushing a shopping cart, to more complex situations like the propulsion of a rocket in space. In the absence of frictional or external forces, the momentum of the shopping cart and the person pushing the shopping cart is conserved. Similarly, in the vacuum of space, the momentum of the ejected rocket fuel and the rocket itself is conserved.

The mathematical formulation of this physical principle follows the idea that the initial momentum (before an action) should be equal to the final momentum (after the action). *Mathematically, this can be expressed as:*

$\Sigma P(\text{initial}) = \Sigma P(\text{final})$

Where ΣP indicates the total or sum of momentum.

If we consider a two-object system where object 1 and object 2 interact, the principle of conservation of momentum can be mathematically modelled as:

$(m1*u1 + m2*u2) = (m1*v1 + m2*v2)$

Here, m1 and m2 denote the masses of object 1 and object 2, respectively. u1 and u2 represent their initial velocities, and v1 and v2 symbolise their final velocities post interaction.

Conservation of Momentum is closely related to Newton's Third Law of Motion, stating that every action has an equal and opposite reaction. This makes greater sense when considering the momentum of colliding objects in closed systems, the total momentum of the system remains conserved, and the change in momentum of one object is mirrored by an equal and opposite change in momentum of the other object.

Appreciating the principle of Conservation of Momentum imparts a thorough understanding of phenomena in diverse fields such as astrophysics, particle physics, and even in engineering applications. By providing us with the ability to predict the results of collisions and interactions, and deciphering many phenomena around us, the Conservation of Momentum makes its significance undisputed in the sphere of physics.

Inertial Frames of Reference

In the field of physics, the concept of 'Frame of Reference' plays a pivotal role in understanding how various observations and calculations are made. At the fundamental level, the Frame of Reference can be understood as a system of abstract coordinate axes that help in depicting the motion or position of an object in space. More specifically, one type of frame, the Inertial Frame of Reference, aids in understanding a unique form of motion which complies with Newton's laws of motion.

The term "inertial", essentially is derived from the concept of inertia, an inherent resistance to changes in motion or state of rest, as per Newton's first law of motion. Therefore, technically, an Inertial Frame of Reference can be perceived as a frame, (itself being at rest or in linear motion), in which bodies at rest or in linear motion continue in their state until another force acts on them.

Regarding the mathematical formulation of the Inertial Frame of Reference, it is built on a profound mechanism of Coordinate Transformation. The fundamental principle behind this idea is that the laws of physics should retain their form across different inertial frames. A critical element in this formulation is the Galilean Transformation, often employed in classical physics which don't account for relativistic effects.

The Galilean transformation mathematically maps the coordinates (x, y, z, t) in one inertial frame to coordinates (x', y', z', t') in another, applying the following algebraic expressions:

$$x' = x - vt$$

$$y' = y$$

$$z' = z$$

$$t' = t$$

where, v is the relative velocity between the reference frames.

In this context, it is intriguing to note how the theory of relativity introduced by Albert Einstein required us to modify the Galilean transformation to accurately describe high-speed scenarios, especially ones approaching the speed of light. In Special Relativity, the Lorentz Transformation replaces the Galilean Transformation, with the following set of equations:

$$x' = \gamma(x - vt)$$

$$t' = \gamma(t - vx/c^2)$$

$$y' = y$$

$$z' = z$$

Here, v is again the relative velocity, c is the speed of light, and γ is the Lorentz Factor defined as $1/\sqrt{(1 - v2/c2)}$.

Inertial Frames of Reference provide an indispensable tool to unveil the laws of nature. Their mathematical formulation, from Galilean transformations to Lorentz transformations, has paved the way for a broader understanding of the physical world, not just on the earthly scale, but on the cosmic scale as well.

Potential Energy and Kinetic Energy

Traditionally, energy has been categorised into two key forms: potential energy and kinetic energy. This dichotomy is a foundational concept in physics, governing our understanding of all physical systems, from the largest celestial bodies to the smallest particles.

Potential energy, in simplistic terms, is the energy that is stored in a system due to its position or configuration. It is the energy a system possesses as a result of being in a certain state. Examples of potential energy in the everyday world include energy stored within a stretched spring, or energy possessed by an object raised above ground level. The most fundamental types of potential energy routinely encountered in physics include gravitational potential energy and elastic potential energy.

Mathematically, potential energy (PE) is given by the formula PE = mgh, where 'm' represents the mass of the object, 'g' denotes the acceleration due to gravity, and 'h' refers to the height above the ground. In terms of elastic potential energy, it can be represented as $PE = 1/2\,kx^2$ where 'k' represents the spring constant and 'x' denotes the amount of displacement from a rest position.

Kinetic energy, on the other hand, is the energy a body or system possesses due to its motion. When an object is in motion, it has the capability to do work and thus carry out transformations of energy. Examples of kinetic energy in action can be found in a myriad of natural phenomena, such as in falling water, wind, and moving animals or vehicles.

Mathematically, kinetic energy (KE) is calculated using the formula $KE = 1/2\,mv^2$, where 'm' is the mass of the object and 'v' is its velocity. This formula reveals that the kinetic energy of an object is proportional to the square of its velocity. Thus, even a small increase in speed can lead to a significant increase in kinetic energy.

The two forms of energy are intrinsically related through the principle of conservation of energy, which states that energy cannot be created or destroyed but only transformed from one form to another. This principle involves the easing transition of potential to kinetic energy and vice versa. For instance, the energy stored in a stretched bow (potential energy) transforms into energy in motion when the bow is released, propelling the arrow forward (kinetic energy).

Work and Energy

Understanding physical behaviours is essential in various domains, from mechanics to thermodynamics. Two elemental concepts in these fields are 'work' and 'energy.' These concepts are interlinked and crucial in defining the operations of systems and instruments in real-life instances. The mathematical formulations of work and energy provide the foundational knowledge necessary for comprehending these principles in detail.

Work

In simple terms, work is identified as the transfer of energy. Explicitly, work is performed by a force on an object that moves. The mathematical formulation of work (W) is expressed as the product of force (F) and displacement (d):

$$W = F.d$$

This formula means that work is equivalent to the force multiplied by the displacement along the direction of the force. However, work is only done when there is a component of the force in the direction of the motion. Therefore, a zero amount of work is done if the displacement is zero, or if the force is perpendicular to the direction of motion.

Energy

Energy, in physics, is defined as the capacity to do work. There are different forms of energy: kinetic, potential, thermal, chemical, electrical, electromagnetic, and nuclear.

One fundamental form, kinetic energy (K), is associated with the motion of an object.

The formula for kinetic energy is as follows:

K = 0.5mv^2

Where 'm' is the mass of the object, and 'v' is its velocity. This formula implies that the kinetic energy is directly proportional to the square of the velocity, meaning that as the velocity of the object doubles, the kinetic energy quadruples.

Potential energy (U), on the other hand, is related to an object's position or state. The equation for potential energy, related to the height of an object in the Earth's gravitational field is expressed as follows:

U = mgh

Where 'm' is the mass of the object, 'g' is the acceleration due to gravity, and 'h' is the height above the ground. This formula suggests that potential energy increases with increasing height, mass, and gravity.

The Law of Conservation of Energy

Energy can neither be created nor destroyed; it can only be transferred or changed from one form to another. This principle, known as the law of conservation of energy, is a cornerstone of physics. The mathematical representation of this law in the context of kinetic and potential energy is often written as follows:

$$K_1 + U_1 = K_2 + U_2$$

Where K_1 and U_1 are the initial kinetic and potential energies, respectively, and K_2 and U_2 are the final kinetic and potential energies, respectively. The formula indicates that the total energy in an isolated system remains constant, implying the energy is conserved.

Angular Momentum

Angular momentum is an intriguing subject in classical mechanics that reveals profound significance about the physics of rotation. An essential concept in both classical and quantum mechanics, angular momentum pertains to the rotational equivalent of a linear momentum but captures a broader range of physical phenomena.

At its core, angular momentum represents the propensity of rotating bodies to continue spinning unless an external force interferes. It is linked to the principles of conservation, especially when the external net torque is equal to zero, leading to constant angular momentum. To understand this further, studying its mathematical formulation becomes inevitable.

Angular Momentum Formulation

The general formulation for angular momentum or "L", for an object of mass "m" moving with velocity "v" in a radius "r", is mathematically expressed as -

$$L = mvr \sin \vartheta$$

In this equation, "θ" symbolises the angle between the velocity vector (v) and the line joining the origin of the coordinate system (O) to the point where the mass is located. However, while considering more complex systems, the vector-based or cross-product formulation of angular momentum simplifies the calculation. This equation is given as:

$$L = r \, x \, p$$

where "p" symbolises the linear momentum of the particle, and the symbol (x) denotes the cross product.

In this context, cross-product enables us to determine the direction of the angular momentum further. Following the right-hand rule, the angular momentum vector is always perpendicular to the plane that the 'r' vector and the 'p' vector reside on.

Rotational Inertia and Angular Momentum

During rotation, mass exhibits resistance to changes, known as rotational or angular inertia (I), and is calculated via the integral over all mass elements (dm) in a rotating body.

$$I = \int r^2 \, dm$$

This resistance becomes a crucial component when exploring the momentum for rotating systems. If ω represents the angular velocity, we can state the angular momentum equation for a rotating object as:

$$L = I\omega$$

Quite similar to Newton's second law for linear motion, this equation shows the relation between angular momentum and angular velocity. Importantly, when there is a net external torque (τ) acting on the system, the resulting change in angular momentum is proportional to the applied torque and the time interval (Δt) over which it acts:

$$\tau = \Delta L / \Delta t$$

Conservation of Angular Momentum

One of the significant principles associated with angular momentum is its conservation. In a closed system, when the net external torque is zero, the total angular momentum remains constant. This law manifests itself in various phenomena, from the spinning of an ice skater to the rotation of celestial bodies, and has far-reaching implications in astrophysics and quantum mechanics.

Angular Momentum in Quantum Mechanics

Angular momentum finds its crucial association in quantum mechanics as well. Quantum mechanical systems demand a distinct treatment, leading to two kinds of angular momentum, namely orbital and spin angular momentum. The former resembles classical angular momentum but with quantization applied, and the latter represents an inherently quantum mechanical property with no classical analogue.

Harmonic and Damped Oscillators

In the observation and study of physical systems and phenomena, physics presents two significant systems: Harmonic and Damped Oscillators. The mathematical models integral to these two systems help us understand an array of natural events, from molecular vibrations and oscillations in pendulums to energy dissipation in car suspensions.

Harmonic Oscillators

A harmonic oscillator is a system that, when displaced from its equilibrium position, experiences a restoring force proportional to the displacement. The simplest mathematical representation of a harmonic oscillator stems from Hooke's Law (F = -kx), where 'F' is the restoring force, 'k' is the spring constant, and 'x' is the displacement from equilibrium. Solving the second order differential equation, md^2x/dt^2 = -kx, provides the standard form solution, x(t) = A cos(ωt + φ), where 'ω' is the angular frequency, 'A' is the amplitude, and 'φ' is the phase constant. This solution captures the essence of the harmonic oscillator: an oscillation at a specific equilibrium point characterised by constancy in amplitude and frequency.

Damped Harmonic Oscillators

While a harmonic oscillator assumes infinite oscillations, the reality is far different. Most physical systems experience damping, a phenomenon where oscillations gradually diminish due to factors like friction and resistance. This damping effect is mathematically represented in damped harmonic oscillators.

The velocity term added to the harmonic oscillator model is the damping force proportional to the velocity (F = -b(dx/dt)). The differential equation md^2x/dt^2 + b(dx/dt) + kx = 0 illustrates this, where 'b' is the damping constant. Solving this differential equation depends on the discriminant, b^2 - 4mk. Suppose the discriminant is less than zero, rapidly leading to complex roots and an under damped system. The system then oscillates in an exponential envelope. Suppose the discriminant equals zero, it results in a critically damped system. Finally, the discriminant greater than zero results in an over damped system where there are no oscillations.

Mathematical Overview

The mathematical notions of harmonic and damped harmonic oscillators are integral to scientists and engineers as they allow the simplification of complex systems. Virtually every structure or machinery involving mechanical vibrations can find its behaviour study benefits from these mathematical models.

Systems of Particles

The subject of systems of particles constitutes a significant area of study in the much broader domain of Physics. Conceptually, a system of particles refers to an assembly of a fixed number of particles, their configuration specified by the positions of particles in space. This system's distinct behaviour determines the physical laws that govern its motion and other physical phenomena. Studying systems of particles is integral to understanding the underlying principles of Mechanics, Thermodynamics, and Quantum Physics.

Mathematically, a system of particles is represented by the positions and velocities of the constituent particles. The state of a system is determined by these particles' positions and momenta, forming a phase space whose points represent the possible states of the system. Thus, the formulation provides a comprehensive view of the system at every moment.

The mathematical formulation of systems of particles involves the use of equations. These equations describe the system's dynamics or changes over time. The fundamental equation formulating a system of particles' dynamics is Newton's second law. It gives us the sum of forces acting on a particle as the product of its mass and acceleration. When this formulation is applied to a system of particles, it gives us an equation representing the total momentum of the system.

Momentum conservation, a critical principle derived from Newton's laws of motion, contributes significantly to the mathematical treatment of a system of particles. It states that the total linear momentum of a system remains constant unless an external force acts on it. The equation for momentum conservation can be derived from Newton's second law, enriching our understanding of the interactions within a system of particles.

To delve deeper, statistical mechanics further extends the analysis on systems of particles by studying the statistical behaviour of assemblies of a large number of particles. A critical concept in this realm is the Maxwell-Boltzmann distribution, which describes the distribution of microscopic particles' speeds in a system at equilibrium.

The mathematical formulation of a system of particles, hence, brings forth an analytical tool to predict and comprehend the system's behaviour. It amalgamates physical concepts and mathematical principles to give a detailed understanding of the system's dynamics at both micro and macro levels.

Lagrangian Mechanics

Lagrangian mechanics, a branch of analytical mechanics, is a subject that has significantly shaped the field of theoretical physics. Named after Joseph-Louis Lagrange, an 18th-century mathematician and astronomer, Lagrangian mechanics presents an intricate structure of mechanical systems using a unique approach by extending the concepts of Newton's laws of motion.

In a basic sense, Lagrangian mechanics can be construed as a reformulation of classical mechanics that predicts the movement of particles. It applies principles derived from calculus of variations to analyse the paths that a system might take to move from one physical state to another. This combination of physics and mathematical principles is centrally disposed towards a distinctive quantity designated as the 'Lagrangian.'

The Lagrangian, denoted as L, is customarily defined as the difference between kinetic energy (T) and potential energy (V) i.e., $L = T-V$. The Lagrangian function represents the total energy of the system under study at any time t, allowing the concept of energy conservation to be developed mathematically. Besides energy conservation, using the Lagrangian function facilitates the determination of a system's trajectory over time through applying the principle of least action.

The principle of least action asserts that the path taken by a physical system between an initial and final state is the one for which the action is minimised. Action, symbolised by S, is computed as the time integral of the Lagrangian. In mathematical terms, it is articulated as: $S = \int L \, dt$.

Central to the Lagrangian formulation is the Euler-Lagrange equation. This equation is a second-order differential equation derived from minimising the action. Applied generally, the Euler-Lagrange equation offers a broader perspective on physical phenomena and caters for many more situations than Newton's laws alone. This equation is formulated as: $d/dt(dL/dv) - dL/dq = 0$, where q signifies the generalised coordinates, and v denotes their time derivatives.

While Newton's laws consider the forces acting upon an object, Lagrangian mechanics shifts the focus to energy, describing the evolution of a physical system in terms of its kinetic and potential energy. This modification permits an inclusive and more generalised analysis of more complex systems. Correspondingly, the Lagrangian approach is prevalent in various physics sub-branches, particularly quantum and statistical mechanics, classical field theory, and notably, the examination of the mechanical behaviour of particles in high-energy particle physics.

Despite being mathematically more sophisticated, the Lagrangian mechanics has several advantages. It can describe systems with varying mass, non-conservative systems, and holonomic and non-holonomic systems efficiently. Moreover, it is more convenient and applicable for systems with variable configurations or constraints, which are hard to treat within the confines of Newtonian mechanics.

Hamiltonian Mechanics

Hamiltonian mechanics represents a reformulation of classical mechanics that is principally known for its utility in theoretical physics. Named after Irish mathematician and physicist Sir William Rowan Hamilton, Hamiltonian mechanics fundamentally pivots on the concept of energy, providing a robust framework that has shaped our understanding of particle dynamics, quantum mechanics, and statistical mechanics.

His equations of motion mirror Newton's in a way that is different but entirely equivalent. Hamilton proposed this new formulation in his work titled "On a General Method in Dynamics" (1834), which was a departure from the force-oriented Newtonian mechanics. The essence of Hamilton's scheme was the introduction of two new concepts in physics: the Hamiltonian and phase space.

The Hamiltonian, denoted by H, is a function of coordinates and momenta, usually described as the total energy of the system. It is expressed as the sum of the kinetic and potential energies (T and V respectively), that is, $H = T + V$. The behaviour and evolution of the physical system are governed by the Hamiltonian function.

Meanwhile, phase space is a manifold where each point defines the state of a physical system. For a system with N particles in three dimensions, the phase space is a 6N-dimensional space, with 3N coordinates to represent the position and 3N coordinates for the momentum.

These come as a pair of first-order differential equations: $\dot{x}$ = $\partial H/\partial p$ and $\dot{p}$ = - $\partial H/\partial x$ (where x and p represent the position and momentum respectively, and the dot represents derivative with respect to time). These equations dictate how the states in the phase space change over time.

The utility of Hamiltonian mechanics is explicitly apparent in quantum mechanics. The Schrödinger equation, the cornerstone of quantum mechanics, can be garnered directly from the Hamiltonian. Moreover, the Dirac and Klein-Gordon equations, prerequisites for the introduction of quantum field theories, are built from relativistic Hamiltonians.

Furthermore, Hamiltonian mechanics contributes significantly to statistical mechanics. Liouville's theorem, stating that the phase space distribution of a Hamiltonian system is constant along the trajectories of the system, is derived from Hamiltonian formalism. Thus, this theoretical structure is central to understanding not only deterministic mechanics but also probabilistic theories.

Collisions

Collisions describe phenomena involving two bodies that interact during a specified period. A study of collisions provides invaluable insights into numerous natural and laboratory-created physical events. In mathematics, collisions are characterised according to their elastic or inelastic nature and can be effectively described using concepts from calculus, algebra, and more sophisticated mathematical domains.

Elastic collisions involve interactions where the total kinetic energy of the involved system is conserved before and after the event. This makes them a particularly interesting case to analyse. From Newton's second law and the conservation principle, two critical equations can be obtained in an elastic collision's mathematical formulation. These equations represent the momentum and energy conservation during the collision, respectively, as described by the equations:

p1_ini + p2_ini = p1_fin + p2_fin

E1_ini + E2_ini = E1_fin + E2_fin

In these equations, 'p' denotes the momentum of a body, 'E' signifies kinetic energy, 'ini' indicates initial, and 'fin' denotes final.

On the other hand, inelastic collisions are characterised by energy dissipation during the collision event. A prime example of this is a car crash, where sound energy is released upon the vehicles' impact. While energy is not conserved, momentum remains conserved in these collisions. Hence, the following equation can be derived to describe inelastic collisions:

p1_ini + p2_ini = (m1 + m2) * V_fin,

where 'm' denotes mass and 'V' stands for velocity.

These equations form the cornerstone of many collision-related simulations and real-life predictions made in fields as varied as astrophysics, traffic modelling, and molecular physics. The mathematical formulation of collisions is instrumental in understanding and predicting the motions and behaviours of the bodies involved in the collisions, enabling us to optimally use and control the mechanics behind everyday events.

However, it is important to remember that the mathematical formulation of collisions is based on several assumptions like perfect rigidity and absence of external forces. In reality, these assumptions may not always hold. Consequently, these classical equations have their limitations and are not universally applicable.

Chaos Theory

Inventoried as a major development in mathematics and physics, Chaos Theory epitomises the complexity in apparently chaotic systems. With its roots traced back to the early 20th century, this theory has gained significant attention leading to advancements in several disciplines.

The crux of Chaos Theory underpins the nuances of dynamical systems highly sensitive to initial conditions. The phenomenon, known as the Butterfly Effect, was conceived by Edward Lorenz in the 1960s while examining atmospheric models. He discovered that even diminutive changes in the initial conditions could lead to vast discrepancies in outcomes. This sensitivity intimates that patterns initially seen as random and disordered may have an underlying deterministic progression, one which is challenging to forecast due to this sensitivity.

Lorenz's work opened the door for a new perspective on the idea of deterministic systems. In deterministic chaos, an elementary system of equations have solutions that never recur or settle down into a cycle, they remain chaotic yet deterministic. Even with known fundamental laws, the unpredictable nature of these systems emerges, rendering them a profound interest within the realms of mathematics and physics.

Mathematically, chaos explores non-linear dynamical systems. They are often examined utilising iterative processes that track the evolution of a system over time. A commonly used tool includes phase space plots which serve as a multidimensional graph plotting variables that define the state of the system, offering visual representations of its trajectory.

One profound mathematical system that illustrates the essence of chaos, is the logistic map formula: $X_{n+1} = rX_n(1 - X_n)$. In this formula, 'r' signifies the parameter, exhibiting how the growth rate influences population dynamics, and 'Xn' denotes the population at time 'n'. When 'r' values change, the system shows dramatically varied behaviour, starting from convergence towards a single value, moving onto a period doubling leading to chaos. The bifurcation diagrams of the logistic map illustrate how stable solutions can fracture into chaotic behaviours as parameters shift.

Laws of Thermodynamics

The study of the Laws of Thermodynamics pertains to the fundamental principles that govern energy transformations and exchanges within physical systems. These laws establish a framework for understanding and analysing various natural phenomena, ranging from the behaviour of gases to chemical reactions and even biological processes.

The Zeroth Law of Thermodynamics

The Zeroth Law of Thermodynamics is a fundamental principle of thermodynamics that sets the groundwork for the concept of temperature, thereby enabling us to compare and quantify thermal energy. According to this law, if two separate systems are in thermal equilibrium with a third system, then they are also in equilibrium with each other. This law essentially serves as the foundation for the numerical scale of temperature.

The Zeroth Law is usually attributed to the eminent physicist Ralph H. Fowler, who added the term to the traditional list of laws to denote its fundamental and primary importance. Despite being the last to be formulated, it is known as 'Zeroth' because it underpins the entire edifice of thermodynamics, thus should have logically preceded the first, second, and third laws.

Mathematically, the Zeroth Law of Thermodynamics can be conceptualised through three systems, A, B, and C. If A is in thermal equilibrium with C, and B is also in thermal equilibrium with C, then by the application of the Zeroth Law, A must be in thermal equilibrium with B. This can be represented mathematically as follows; if A=C and B=C, then A=B. This seemingly simple mathematical representation is a powerful tool, providing the basis for developing the concept of empirical temperature.

Both empirical and absolute temperature scales are based on the Zeroth Law of thermodynamics. Empirical scales use observable phenomena like the expansion of a gas or liquid under heat to measure temperature changes. In contrast, the absolute temperature scale, founded on kinetic theory and statistical mechanics, provides an accurate and universal measure of temperature irrespective of the type of matter or the processes it undergoes.

The concept of empirical temperature in thermodynamics is primarily born from the Zeroth Law. It states that if two systems are in thermal equilibrium, their empirical temperatures must be equal. The empirical temperature of an arbitrary system can hence be defined by establishing its equilibrium with a standard reference system and then quantifying the property of the reference system.

Practical implications of the Zeroth Law include its use in developing thermometers and calibrating temperature scales. For example, mercury-in-glass thermometers exploit the property of mercury expansion under heat. By establishing an empirical correlation between mercury's volume and the state of a reference system (like the freezing and boiling points of water), an empirical temperature scale can be devised.

The First Law of Thermodynamics

The First Law of Thermodynamics, often described as the Law of Energy Conservation, stipulates that energy can be neither created nor destroyed in an isolated system. Instead, it can only be converted from one form to another.

From a physical perspective, it implies that the total energy within an isolated system preserves well-defined specificity, irrespective of the sort of processes taking place within that system. In essence, while the system may undergo chemical reactions or changes in physical states, the initial energy is accurately transposed to balance the final energy state.

Mathematically, the First Law of Thermodynamics can be expressed in various ways, with each aimed at representing distinctive conditions or perspectives. One commonly used expression of this law in a closed system undergoing a thermodynamic cycle is:

$$\Delta U = Q - W$$

In this expression, ΔU refers to the change in internal energy of the system, Q represents the heat absorbed by the system, and W signifies the work done by the system. Essentially, it conceptualises that any increment in the energy of a system should be equal to the amount of energy added to the system by heat, minus the amount lost through work done by the system.

Applied in an infinitesimal (differential form), the equation becomes:

$$dU = \delta Q - \delta W$$

It signifies that an infinitesimal increase in the internal energy (dU) of a system equals an infinitesimally small quantity of heat added to the system (δQ), minus an infinitesimally small amount of work done by the system (δW).

However, it is critical to note that this law merely states the energy conservation principle without elucidating the direction of the probable transformation, which is covered by the Second Law of Thermodynamics. Besides, the first law does not distinguish between the microscopic and macroscopic forms of energy.

The Second Law of Thermodynamics

The Second Law of Thermodynamics denotes that the total entropy, a measure of disorder or randomness, in an isolated system can only increase over time. Simply put, it states that energy cannot flow from a cooler object to a hotter object independently. The heat energy will naturally move from a hot body to a cold body without external forces applied.

Furthermore, the law showcases the irreversible nature of the majority of natural phenomena. The cogency of the Second

Law is manifest in various fields, from statistical interpretation, the phenomena of irreversibility, engine efficiency, to cosmic thermodynamics and the paradox of the black hole thermodynamics.

Exploring the mathematical formulations of the Second Law, we note two primary formulations: the Clausius statement and the Kelvin-Planck statement.

The Clausius statement, named after Rudolf Clausius who formulated the law, specifies that it is impossible for any process to solely transfer heat from a body at a low temperature to a body at a higher temperature. The mathematical representation of the statement, $\Delta S \geq Q/T$, where ΔS is the change in the entropy of the system, Q is the heat transferred and T is the absolute temperature, captures the essence of this principle.

The Kelvin-Planck statement, proposed by Lord Kelvin and Max Planck, asserts that no cyclic process can withdraw heat from a reservoir and convert it entirely into work. Mathematically, it gives birth to the inequality $1 - T_c/T_h \leq \eta \leq 1$, where η is the efficiency of a heat engine, T_c is the temperature of the cold reservoir and T_h is the temperature of the hot reservoir.

The Second Law has deep implications in multiple domains, including quantum mechanics, cosmology, and information theory. Understanding this law and its mathematical representation helps demystify the elements of our universe and their intrinsic interactions.

It is essential to note that the potential energy within a closed system is not typically converted entirely into useful work, thanks to this law. Most energy is dissipated as unusable energy, establishing the distinction between usable and unusable energy that resonates with the Second Law of Thermodynamics.

The Third Law of Thermodynamics

The Third Law of Thermodynamics, a critical component of physical chemistry, establishes that the entropy of a perfect crystal at absolute zero is exactly equal to zero. Nobel laureate Walter Nernst first proposed this law in 1906, providing a foundational postulate for further scientific exploration and the understanding of physical constants like entropy and absolute zero.

The Third Law of Thermodynamics can be articulated both qualitatively and quantitatively. Its qualitative formulation states, "As a perfect crystal's temperature critically approaches absolute zero, the entropy, denoted by S, approximates a minimum constant value." The crux of this statement gravitates towards the natural tendency of a system to obtain minimum energy, reaching an orderly arrangement at absolute zero.

Quantitatively, the Third Law of Thermodynamics is usually stated as $\Delta S = 0$ at $T = 0$, where ΔS is the change in entropy and T is the temperature. This expression signifies an ideally perfect crystal state with zero entropy at absolute zero temperature. Realistically, this is theoretical because reaching absolute zero is practically unattainable due to the unlikeliness of perfectly regular atomic arrangement.

The law's mathematical formulation anchors on the concept of entropy. The fundamental definition of entropy involves heat transfer (q) divided by temperature (T): $\Delta S = q/T$. Importantly, entropy is a state function only dependent on initial and final states and not on the path taken. The mathematical representation, $S = k_B \ln W$, where k_B is the Boltzmann constant and W is the number of microstates, excavates into the statistical underpinnings of entropy.

A significant consequence of the Third Law of Thermodynamics is the inability to reach absolute zero temperature by any finite number of processes. Calculations following Carnot cycles and the limitation of the efficiency of heat engines assert that constant-cooling operations, however repeated, cannot bring a system to absolute zero. This aspect has profound implications in low-temperature physics and quantum computing, straining the pursuit of absolute zero to glean quantum supremacy and step change in computational capabilities.

Carnot Cycle and the Efficiency of Heat Engines

Understanding the mechanisms that govern the efficiency of heat engines forms an integral part of thermodynamics, one of the branches of physical sciences. A key concept in this regard is the Carnot Cycle, a theoretical construct proposed by Sadi Carnot in 1824 that sets the upper limit on the efficiency of any heat engine operating between two given temperatures.

The Carnot Cycle operates under the optic of idealised assumptions including reversibility and absence of dissipative effects. The cycle is characterised by two isothermal and two adiabatic processes that occur cyclically. The cycle starts with an isothermal expansion, followed by an adiabatic expansion, and then an isothermal compression. The last phase of the cycle is an adiabatic compression, returning the cycle to its initial state. This combination of four processes ensures there is cyclical reversibility.

The isothermal processes, meaning they occur at a constant temperature, involve heat exchange between the system (heat engine) and the environment. During isothermal expansion, the system absorbs heat from the higher temperature reservoir, and then, during the isothermal compression phase, rejects heat into a lower temperature reservoir.

In the adiabatic processes, the system is considered to be perfectly insulated, thus preventing any heat exchange with the environment. The adiabatic compression phase involves an increase in gas temperature, while the adiabatic expansion phase involves a decrease.

Efficiency is central to the workings of the Carnot Cycle. The efficiency (η) of a heat engine is defined as the work done (W) by the heat engine divided by the heat absorbed from the hot reservoir (Qh).

Mathematically, the efficiency of a Carnot engine can be expressed as $\eta = 1- (Tc/Th)$, where Tc and Th are the absolute temperatures of the cold and hot reservoirs, respectively. It's important to note that these temperatures must be in Kelvin for the formula to hold. This equation defines the maximum possible efficiency for any heat engine operating between these two temperatures.

The main take away from Carnot's theorem is that no real heat engine operating between two energy reservoirs can be more efficient than a Carnot engine operating between the same reservoirs. This elegant theorem provides a way of rating the performance of all heat engines. It allows engineers to understand that all real heat engines have efficiencies less than 100% due to unavoidable heat losses to the environment.

However, in reality, no engine is truly Carnot efficient, since all engines feature irreversible processes such as friction and turbulence, along with other forms of energy dissipation.

The Role of Temperature in Thermodynamics

At the heart of this discipline, temperature plays an indispensable role, functioning as the measure of the average kinetic energy in a system. It is the magnitude of internal energy, proportional to the average kinetic energy of the system. Temperature quantifies the direction of energy flow between systems, dictating the movement of heat from a region of a higher temperature to one of lower temperature.

In thermodynamics, the first law postulates the conservation of energy. It mathematically articulates that the change in the internal energy of a system is equal to the heat added to the system minus the work done by the system. This establishes the concept of heat as a form of energy transfer, where temperature plays the principal role of the driving force behind this transfer. Further, the second law of thermodynamics elaborates on the principle of energy degradation, through which it communicates that the entropy of an isolated system always increases, a process again determined by temperature.

This quantitative measure is also pivotal in phase transitions, such as the transformations from solid to liquid, liquid to gas, and so forth. The critical temperatures at which these phase transitions occur: such as the boiling point or melting point, are crucial in assessing and controlling numerous everyday processes and scientific experiments. Thus, the understanding and accurate measurement of temperature are arguably the cornerstones of practical thermodynamics.

In a broader sense, the role of temperature as a determining factor for performance and efficiency underlies its importance. In a heat engine, for example, the temperature difference between the heat source (the high-temperature reservoir) and the heat sink (the low-temperature reservoir) governs the maximum possible work output or, equivalently, the minimum work input for refrigeration.

Mathematically, temperature is incorporated into several thermodynamic identities, including the ideal gas law PV=nRT, where T denotes temperature. Herein, R is the ideal gas constant, P is pressure, V is volume, and n is the number of moles of the gas.

Equilibrium and Thermodynamic Processes

Equilibrium in a thermodynamic system occurs when the system's macroscopic observable properties do not change over time. In thermodynamics, equilibrium is achieved when a system's properties such as pressure (P), temperature (T), and volume (V), remain constant. Mathematically, it can be expressed as $dP = dT = dV = 0$. This principle is further expounded through the zeroth law of thermodynamics, which states that if two thermodynamic systems are each in equilibrium with a third one, then they are in equilibrium with each other.

Thermodynamic processes refer to the various changes a system can experience. Four key processes are distinguished: isothermal (constant temperature), isobaric (constant pressure), isochoric (constant volume), and adiabatic (there's no heat flow in or out of the system)

In isothermal processes, the temperature remains constant ($dT = 0$). The work done (W) in this process can be represented by the formula $W = nRT \ln(Vf/Vi)$, where n is the number of moles, R is the universal gas constant, and Vf and Vi represent the final and initial volumes, respectively.

In isobaric processes, the pressure remains constant ($dP = 0$). For the work done in such cases, the formula used is $W = P(Vf - Vi)$.

Isochoric processes keep the volume constant ($dV = 0$). In this situation, the work done is $W = 0$, since no volume change means no work is done.

For adiabatic processes (no heat transfer), by setting the first law of thermodynamics ($\Delta Q = \Delta U + W$) to $\Delta Q = 0$, the formula for the work done becomes $W = -\Delta U$.

Ideal Gas Laws and Thermodynamics

Ideal Gas Laws relate the variables of state, including pressure (P), volume (V), temperature (T), and the quantity (n) for a hypothetical gas termed as an 'ideal' or 'perfect' gas. An ideal gas conforms entirely to these laws at all conditions of temperature and pressure.

The laws consist of three basic principles: Boyle's Law, Charles's Law, and Avogadro's Law. Boyle's Law states that pressure and volume of a gas have an inverse relationship when the temperature is held constant; therefore, an increase in pressure would result in a decrease in volume. Charles's Law, on the other hand, establishes that if pressure is kept constant, the volume of an ideal gas is directly proportional to its temperature. The third law named after Avogadro postulates that equal volumes of gases at the same temperature and pressure contain equal numbers of molecules, a premise that enables the calculation of a gas's molecular weight.

However, since no gas can be truly 'ideal' or 'perfect', deviations occur at high pressure and low temperature, leading to the introduction of the Van der Waals equation, a modification to the Ideal Gas Law.

The relationship between the Ideal Gas Laws and the law of thermodynamics is also noteworthy. Thermodynamics pertains to the study of energy, heat, and work. The First Law of Thermodynamics emphasises that energy cannot be created or destroyed merely transferred or transformed. In terms of ideal gases, it's displayed in the interchange of kinetic energy (heat) and potential energy (work) during isothermal expansion or compression processes.

The Second Law of Thermodynamics, on the other hand, connotes the inevitable increase of entropy (disorder) in isolated systems. In the context of gases, this reveals that gas molecules dispersed in a container will naturally spread out over time.

Statistical Thermodynamics and the Role of Microstates

In statistical thermodynamics, a microstate refers to a particular configuration of the constituent particles in a system. These particles, usually atoms or molecules, can be in different positions and have different velocities, leading to different microstates. When systems comprising a significant number of particles, say about 10^23, are considered, there exist an incredibly massive number of possible microstates.

Key to statistical thermodynamics is an assumption referred to as the equiprobability postulate. This states that in equilibrium, all microstates of a system are equally probable. This implies that for an isolated system in equilibrium, all the accessible microstates have equal probabilities of occurrence.

Entropy and Microstates:

One of the key concepts that are intrinsically tied to microstates is entropy, denoted by S. Entropy is a measure of the number of ways particles in a system can be arranged without altering the overall appearance or the macrostate of the system. The concept can be formulated mathematically in terms of microstates as:

$$S = k * \ln(W)$$

Where:

- S = entropy,
- k = Boltzmann's constant,
- W = the number of microstates,
- ln indicates the natural logarithm.

The equation is known as Boltzmann's entropy formula, wherein the entropy of a system is proportional to the natural logarithm of the number of microstates.

Energy and Microstates:

Each microstate of a system has a corresponding energy associated with it. The distribution of energies across the different microstates is given by the Boltzmann distribution:

$$P(E) = (g(E) * e^{(-E/kT)} / Z)$$

Where:

- $P(E)$ = the probability of the system being in a state of energy E,
- $g(E)$ = the number of states with energy E,
- k = Boltzmann constant,
- T = absolute temperature,
- Z = the partition function, given by the summation over all states $g(E) * e^{(-E/kT)}$.

The equation states that the probability of a system being in a particular microstate with energy E is directly proportional to the number of states with that energy and inversely proportional to the exponential of the energy divided by the product of the Boltzmann constant and the absolute temperature.

Principles of Electromagnetism

Electromagnetism is a fundamental branch of physics that examines the interaction between electric charges and magnetic fields. The study of electromagnetism originated in the early 19th century with the innovative work of Hans Christian Ørsted, Michael Faraday, and James Clerk Maxwell. Over time, it has proved crucial in various technological applications including electricity generation and telecommunications.

Central to understanding electromagnetism is the concept of an electromagnetic field. This is a physical field produced by electrically charged objects and time-varying magnetic fields. The electromagnetic field propagates in the form of waves (electromagnetic waves) that move at the speed of light. Maxwell's equations, a set of four differential equations, provide a mathematical description of the electromagnetic field.

Electric Charges and Fields

Electric charges are a basic property of matter. They are either positive, negative, or neutral. Subatomic particles: protons, electrons, and neutrons are the units of the electric charge. Protons carry positive charges, electrons possess negative charges, and neutrons are uncharged. In the context of quantum electrodynamics, the principle of charge conservation states that the total electric charge in an isolated system remains constant.

The mathematical formulation of an electric charge is a straightforward concept. The elementary charge, represented by 'e', is the smallest absolute amount of electric charge that can exist. It is approximately equal to 1.602 x 10^-19 coulombs, and it is the charge possessed by a single proton or -1e is owned by a single electron.

Charged particles exert forces on each other. The electric field is a physical field that surrounds electrically-charged particles and exerts force on other particles. Mathematically defined, the electric field E at a location is the force F that a positive test charge QT would experience at that location divided by the magnitude of the test charge itself, i.e., E = F/QT. Thus, electric fields describe the electric influence of charge distributions.

The mathematical form of Coulomb's Law precisely outlines this concept. According to Coulomb's law, the force F between two point charges q1 and q2 separated by a distance r is F = k * q1 * q2 / r^2, where k is Coulomb's constant, approximately equal to 8.99 * 10^9 N.m^2/C^2. The negative sign indicates that the force is attractive if the charges are of opposite signs and repulsive if the charges have the same sign.

Stemming from this, Gauss's Law mathematically describes electric fields originating from various charge distributions. It states that the total electric flux out of a closed surface is proportional to the charge enclosed by the surface. Mathematically it is represented as $\oint E \cdot dA = Q_{enc}/\varepsilon_0$. Here, E is the electric field, dA is a differential area vector on the Gaussian surface, Qenc is the total charge enclosed, and ε_0 is the permittivity of free space.

Gauss's Law and Ampere's Law

A closer look at Gauss's Law reveals that it stems from the behaviour of electric charges. Gauss's Law states that the total outward electric flux through a closed surface is equal to the total charge enclosed by that surface divided by the electric permittivity. In mathematical terms, it can be written as $\oint E \cdot dA = Q\_enc / \varepsilon\_0$, where E represents the electric field, dA is a differential area, Q_enc is the enclosed electric charge, and ε_0 is the permittivity of free space.

Gauss's Law becomes useful in situations with high symmetry, specifically spherical, cylindrical, and planar symmetry. It is simpler to apply Gauss's Law in these instances than to use Coulomb's Law because it allows the direct calculation of the total electric field without needing to calculate individual field contributions from each charge.

Turning our attention to Ampere's Law, it forms part of Maxwell's Equations, a set of four partial differential equations that form the foundation of classical electrodynamics and optics. Ampere's Law states that the magnetic field in space around an electric current is proportional to the electric current, which serves as its source.

Mathematically, Ampere's law can be represented as $\oint B \cdot dl = \mu 0 \times (I\_enc + \varepsilon 0 \times \partial(\oint E \cdot dA) / \partial t)$. Here, B denotes magnetic field, dl represents a differential length element, I_enc is the current through that loop, and μ_0 is the permeability of free space. The involvement of ε_0 underlies the association of Ampere's Law with displacement current in addition to conduction current.

Thus, Gauss's Law and Ampere's Law, despite their different focus areas, electric fields and magnetic fields, respectively, share the common thread of simplifying complex calculations. Both laws also underscore the interconnected nature of electricity and magnetism, paving the way for the profound realisation of electromagnetism.

Electric Potential and Potential Difference

Electric potential, sometimes referred to as electric field potential, is a measure of the electric potential energy per unit charge. More simply put, it represents the work done by an external force in moving a unit positive charge from a reference point to a specific point in an electric field, without producing an acceleration. The unit of electric potential is the Volt (V).

Equally important, the Potential Difference, often termed Voltage, is the difference in electric potential between two points in an electric field. It specifies the amount of work done to move a unit charge from one place to another against an electric field. Like electric potential, the unit to measure potential difference is also Volt (V).

In an electric circuit for instance, the battery or power supply creates a potential difference. This voltage stimulates the flow of electric charge, or the current, across the circuit. In simpler terms, the potential difference could be thought of as the 'push' that instigates charges to move in a wire.

Furthermore, electric potential is a characteristic of the electric field, a scalar quantity, hence, it does not have a direction. It only has magnitude. The potential at a point in the field is the same in all directions. Under rigid conditions, when the electric potential decreases in the direction of the electric field, we say there is a negative potential gradient.

On the other hand, potential difference isn't associated with a single point. Rather, it involves two different positions in the field. Therefore, it effectively quantifies the work done against the electric forces to 'travel' from one location in the field to another.

Understanding Electric Potential and Potential Difference is critical because these foundations underpin various applications of electricity, from consumer electronics like televisions and cell phones, to large scale power generation and distribution systems. Hence, an appreciation of these concepts is a prerequisite to understanding more advanced topics in electricity and working with electrical systems.

Capacitance, Electric Current and Ohm's Law

Capacitance is a fundamental concept in the study of electronics and electrical engineering. It characterises the capacity of a physical body to store an electrical charge. Usually, capacitance is measured in Farads (F), which are named after the renowned scientist Michael Faraday. Capacitors, ubiquitous in electronic circuits, exploit the potential of capacitance to charge and discharge promptly, thus enabling functions such as energy storage, noise filtering, and signal coupling.

The main principle underlying a capacitor's operation is its ability to store energy in an electric field between two conductive plates separated by an insulating material or dielectric. The amount of charge (Q) the capacitor can store is directly proportional to the voltage (V) applied across the plates, expressed in the form of the equation $Q=CV$, where C represents the capacitance.

An electric current is created by the movement of electrically charged particles. This dynamic flow powers everyday devices, from smartphones and computers to vehicles and domestic appliances. The current measures the rate at which charge flows past a point on a circuit and is expressed in Amperes (A). The two forms of electric current are Direct Current (DC) and Alternating Current (AC). In DC, electric charges flow in a consistent direction, whereas in AC, the flow of charges periodically reverses direction.

At this juncture, it is pertinent to introduce Ohm's Law, which underpins the fundamental relationship between voltage, current, and resistance in an electrical circuit.

Named after the German physicist Georg Ohm, Ohm's law states that the current (I) flowing in a circuit is directly proportional to the voltage (V) and inversely proportional to the resistance (R). This law is commonly depicted by the equation I=V/R.

The importance of Ohm's Law in electrical theory cannot be overemphasised. It dictates design parameters and rules of operations in various electrical and electronic systems. In resistive circuits, Ohm's law simplifies predictive procedures, enabling practitioners to calculate values for voltage, current, or resistance when the other two parameters are known.

Magnetic Forces and Fields

Coulomb's law, relating to electric force, was put forth by Charles Augustin de Coulomb in the 18th century. It states that the force between two electrical charges is directly proportional to the product of their charges and inversely proportional to the square of the distance between them. Mathematically, the force (F) is given by (F=k.q1.q2/r^2), where q1 and q2 are the magnitudes of the charges, r is the distance between charges, and k is the electrostatic constant.

While Coulomb's law provides insights into electrical forces, the Lorentz force law proposed by H. A. Lorentz, explains the force on a charged particle moving in a magnetic field. According to this law, the force (F) experienced by a charge (q) moving at a velocity (v) cross to the magnetic field (B) is given by (F=q.v x B). This cross product implies that the

Lorentz force is perpendicular to both the velocity of the charged particle and the magnetic field direction.

An additional significant law is the principle of superposition which states that, in any system with multiple interacting charges, the net force on a particular charge is merely the vector sum of the forces on it by all individual charges. This principle simplifies the calculations involved in determining the net force in complex systems with multiple charges and magnetic fields.

The mentioned magnetic forces and fields are invisible and exist in a region of space produced by moving electric charges. This region influences other electrically charged particles that are brought into it. The interaction manifests as a force pushing or pulling the particles, referred to as a magnetic force. This is how magnets work on a fundamental level. Calculating magnetic forces and understanding magnetic fields leads to practical applications like electric motors, MRI scans, and data storage devices.

Basic calculations in magnetism revolve around fundamental rules and laws. The direction of the magnetic field and force is defined by the right-hand rule, which states that if the thumb of the right hand points in the direction of conventional current or in the direction of the velocity of a positive charge, the direction that the fingers curl represents the direction of the magnetic field.

The mathematical representation and comprehension of magnetic forces and fields help to visualise and grasp their effects better. These laws and rules have been central to various breakthroughs in technology and scientific research. Critical among them are power generation and transmission, telecommunication systems, electric cars, and medical technologies. Understanding the mathematical aspects of these forces and fields forms an essential part of not just physics but also other branches of science that rely on electromagnetism for functioning and advancements.

Magnetic Flux and Faraday's Law of Induction

Magnetic Flux represents the quantity of the total magnetism or the magnetic field, which passes through a specified area. This concept bridges the gap between magnetism and electricity, forming the basis of various essential electromagnetic devices and principles, including transformers, solenoids, and Faraday's Law of Electromagnetic Induction.

The magnetic flux is quantified using the formula $\Phi = B.A$, where 'B' signifies the magnetic field's strength and 'A' signifies the area. The angle (θ) between the magnetic field and the area vector also plays a significant role, as the magnetic flux is at its maximum when the magnetic field is perpendicular to the area $(\theta=0)$. Consequently, the formula should more accurately be written as $\Phi = B.A.\cos\theta$.

Faraday's Law of Induction, on the other hand, explains how a magnetic field can be converted into electricity and vice versa. Michael Faraday discovered in the 19th century that changing a magnetic field within a closed loop of wire induces a current to flow within that wire. This formed the foundation for the development of electric generators and transformers.

Formally, Faraday's Law is represented as $E = -d\Phi/dt$, in which E is the electromotive force (EMF), $d\Phi$ is the change in magnetic flux, and dt is the change in time. The negative sign is a reflection of Lenz's law, which states that the direction of induced EMF and hence the induced current will oppose the change that causes it.

Mathematically, the total magnetic flux (Φ) through some area (A) can be calculated by integrating the magnetic field (B) over the area. This mathematical representation is evident in Gauss's law for magnetism, $\int B.dA = 0$, stating that for any closed surface, the integral of the magnetic field over the area is equal to zero.

Furthermore, when the magnetic field changes, as per Faraday's Law, an EMF is induced in a circuit, which can be calculated using the formula $E = -N \, \Delta\Phi/\Delta t$, where N is the number of turns in the coil, and $\Delta\Phi/\Delta t$ is the rate of change of magnetic flux.

Electromagnetic Oscillations

Electromagnetic oscillations form a fundamental aspect of electromagnetic theory. In a broad scope, these oscillations are universal phenomena that underlie a broad spectrum of physical systems. Primarily, they constitute the basis for wireless communication technologies we heavily rely on today, such as radio and television.

Firstly, understanding electromagnetic oscillations demands an essential grasp of electromagnetic theory and Maxwell's equations, the bedrock of contemporary electromagnetic phenomena. These mathematical expressions detail the behaviour of electric and magnetic fields, their interrelations, and their correlation with electric charges and currents. They establish the foundation for understanding how electromagnetic fields oscillate.

An electromagnetic oscillation, in its simplest description, refers to the periodic modulation of electric and magnetic fields, characterised by a changing electric field inducing a changing magnetic field, and vice versa. The oscillatory nature of these fields proves crucial for the propagation of electromagnetic waves, thus impinging on wireless communication.

Key to oscillations is the concept of a harmonic oscillator, which can be illustrated by a mass on a spring or a pendulum in a clock, exhibiting a to-and-fro motion. Similarly, when an electric charge oscillates to and from within an antenna, it generates a changing electric field which, in turn, induces a changing magnetic field. The propagation of these changing electric and magnetic fields in space produces electromagnetic waves. It is these waves that carry information in wireless communication systems.

The principles of electromagnetic oscillation find their application in many modern utilities beyond wireless communication, such as electromagnetic spectrum in the form of visible light for sight, infrared for heat, and ultraviolet for skin tanning. Moreover, medical imaging technologies like MRI, and energy production methods like nuclear fusion also leverage the behaviour of electromagnetic oscillations.

The speed at which these oscillations take place can vary immensely, expressed as frequency and measured in Hertz. The electromagnetic spectrum describes the full range of all possible electromagnetic frequencies, from the extremely low-frequency (ELF) waves to very high-frequency gamma rays.

Despite the apparent complexity, understanding electromagnetic oscillations and their broad application scope helps to appreciate the sophistication with which we can manipulate electromagnetic phenomena. Whether it's effortlessly streaming a live video or harnessing nuclear power, it all fundamentally reduces to how effectively we control and use electromagnetic oscillations.

Reflection and Refraction of Electromagnetic Waves

Reflection and refraction are fundamental properties of electromagnetic waves which are crucial to our understanding of the physical world. When an electromagnetic wave encounters a boundary separating two different mediums, it is divided into two parts; one part is reflected back into the initial medium, while the other part progresses into the second medium. This phenomenon is known as reflection.

Reflection obeys the law of reflection, which states that the angle of incidence equals the angle of reflection. It is a straightforward process, providing the foundational understanding for mirrors, fibre optic technology and radar systems, among other applications. The intensity of the reflection depends on the electromagnetic wave frequency and the properties of the interface between the two mediums.

On the contrary, refraction is the bending of an electromagnetic wave as it passes from one medium to another. The law of refraction, also known as Snell's Law, mathematically defines the relationship between the angles of incidence and refraction, considering the velocities of the wave in the two different mediums. Significantly, the manipulation of refractive indices in optical components like lenses, enable the concentration, collimation or dispersion of electromagnetic waves like light.

However, both processes, reflection and refraction, come with their respective caveats. Achieving total reflection requires specific conditions, such as when light traverses from a denser medium, like water, to a less dense medium, like air, at shallow angles. Phenomena such as this can lead to the creation of an optic fibre, where total internal reflection allows light to travel great distances without significant power loss. Similarly, while refraction provides the manipulation of electromagnetic wave paths, high levels of refractive index disparities can result in optical aberrations or distortions.

Polarisation of Electromagnetic Waves

At the root of electromagnetic waves lies the oscillation of both electric and magnetic fields. Both fields oscillate in a plane perpendicular to the direction of propagation, with their peaks and troughs occurring simultaneously. However, our focus is on the electric field vectors, whose properties and changes depict the wave's polarisation. Depending upon the nature of these oscillations or vibrations, we can categorise polarisation into three primary types: linear, circular, and elliptical polarisation.

Linear polarisation, often the simplest to visualise, presents a situation where the electric field vector oscillates in a singular fixed linear plane, perpendicular to the wave's direction of propagation. Natural light is partially linearly polarised; and this principle is at the core of technologies such as LCD screens and polarised sunglasses.

Circular and elliptical polarisation, on the other hand, involve more complex electric field oscillations. In the case of circular polarisation, the electric field vector describing the electromagnetic wave rotates in a particular direction (either clockwise or anti-clockwise), maintaining a constant magnitude. This creates the impression of a helix or screw-type motion.

Elliptical polarisation is the general case of polarised light and engulfs both linear and circular polarisation. Here, the tip of the electric field vector traces out an ellipse in time. The elliptical shape may vary widely, from a line (linear polarisation) to a circle (circular polarisation), depicting the heterogeneous nature of the phenomena.

Understanding the polarisation of electromagnetic waves is more than a theoretical curiosity. It has significant practical applications that impact everyday life. From communication systems to meteorology, remote sensing, astronomy, and even biology, understanding and manipulating the polarisation of light is a gateway to a universe of possibilities. Indeed, many natural and artificial systems respond differently to different polarisations, enabling the separation of signals, measurements of atmospheric constituents, and even the detection of cancerous tissues.

The Nature of Light

Light is one of the most fascinating natural phenomena in the world. It is a form of electromagnetic radiation that is visible to the human eye and is essential for the sustenance of life on Earth. It has a wide range of applications, from photography to communication, and has been studied extensively by scientists for centuries. The nature of light is complex and mysterious, and we are only just beginning to understand its inner workings.

Wave-Particle Duality of Light

The wave-particle duality phenomenon, a cornerstone of quantum mechanics, fundamentally reshaped the scientific understanding of light behaviour. In classical physics, most entities could be identified as either particles or waves. However, quantum mechanics illustrates that light exhibits characteristics of both waves and particles under different situations. This theoretical framework is known as wave-particle duality.

Wave-Particle Duality Overview

Wave-particle duality is a fundamental concept in quantum mechanics, proposing that all particles also exhibit properties of waves. This idea emerged from discussions about light and its characteristics. A wave can be defined as an oscillation that carries energy or information, continually changing place or direction, such as light or sound. Particles, conversely, are defined as small discrete entities with energy, like electrons.

Light as a Wave

In the 1800s, Thomas Young performed a double-slit experiment, which ultimately demonstrated that light travelled as waves. He sent light through two slits, and instead of forming two direct bright spots on the screen behind, an interference pattern appeared: a series of bright and dark fringes. This pattern could only be explained with wave theory, for this interference occurs when peaks of light waves from one slit combine with those from another. When peaks meet troughs, they cancel out, forming dark spaces.

Light as a Particle

The concept of light as a particle, or a 'photon', emerged from the work of Max Planck in 1900 and Albert Einstein in 1905. To explain the phenomenon known as the photoelectric effect, No plain wave explanation could suffice. Einstein proposed that light was made up of packets of energy, called photons. The energy (E) in these photons could be calculated using Planck's constant (h) and frequency (v) in the equation $E = h{*}v$.

Mathematical Applications

The Wavelength of Light

The mathematical relation between wavelength and frequency is expressed by the formula $\lambda v = c$, where "λ" is the wavelength, "v" is the frequency, and "c" is the speed of light. By knowing the frequency or wavelength, we can calculate the other.

Particle Properties: Energy and Momentum

The energy (E) of a particle of light (a photon) is given by $E = h*v$, and its momentum (p) is given by $p = h/\lambda$. Here "h" is Planck's constant. These equations show that light, thought of as a particle, carries energy and momentum.

Complexity of Wave-Particle Duality

The wave-particle duality is not just an 'either/or' principle – it combines the natures of waves and particles. In quantum mechanics, one cannot simultaneously measure both the position (a particle-like property) and momentum (a wave-like property) precisely. This rule, known as the Heisenberg Uncertainty Principle, introduces inherent fuzziness into the positions and trajectories of particles.

Wave-particle duality represents a fundamental departure from old physics by introducing a bold new vision of reality. Quantum mechanics' complex theoretical framework, which includes fascinating concepts like wave-particle duality, has given us unprecedented insight into the most profound and esoteric aspects of the universe.

Reflection and Refraction of Light

Reflection comes into play when light rays change direction after encountering a different medium or boundary. This principle is described by the Law of Reflection which states that the angle of incidence equals the angle of reflection. Eg. If a light ray hits a mirror at an angle of 45 degrees, it will reflect off at the same angle, a 45-degree reflection.

Equally significant is refraction–a concept that explains the bending of light as it travels through different mediums. According to Snell's law, refraction can be mathematically represented by the equation: n1*sin(theta1) = n2*sin(theta2). Here, 'n1' and 'n2' are the refractive indices of the mediums, and 'theta1' and 'theta2' are the angles of incidence and refraction, respectively.

For instance, the refractive index of air is approximately 1, while that of water is approximately 1.333. Therefore, when light travels from air to water at an incidence angle of 30 degrees, the refraction angle can be calculated using Snell's law as approximately 22.08 degrees.

Besides, the principle of refraction also introduces the concept of total internal reflection, where light is completely reflected within a medium, causing light rays to follow a path parallel to the boundary of the medium. This phenomenon is instrumental in the functioning of optical fibres in telecommunication systems.

While both reflection and refraction seem fairly simple to acknowledge, their intricate calculations and practical implementations have laid the foundation for various scientific breakthroughs, from laser systems to medical imaging technologies.

Colour and the Visible Spectrum of Light

Colour constitutes a fundamental aspect of our reality, shaping our perception and providing a rich, visual experience of the world. This complex phenomenon stems from the interaction between light and the human eye, nested within the visible spectrum of light. Given that light's nature is both a particle and a wave, colour arises from the wavelengths of light reflected off surfaces, reaching our eyes and eliciting perceptual responses.

Colour

Colours are subjective perceptual experiences that result from the way specific wavelengths of light stimulate the photoreceptor cells (cones) in our retinas. Humans typically have three types of cones sensitive to short (blue), medium (green), and long (red) wavelengths, leading to our trichromatic colour vision. Each colour we perceive corresponds to a particular range of wavelengths. Red, for example, corresponds to light wavelengths around 700 nm, while violet light corresponds to wavelengths around 400 nm.

Visible Spectrum of Light

The visible spectrum of light, forming a narrow portion of the electromagnetic spectrum, is the range of light wavelengths perceivable by the human eye. It spans wavelengths from approximately 400 nm (violet) to 700nm (red). One can visualise this spectrum as a rainbow, with colours transitioning seamlessly from one to another: violet, indigo, blue, green, yellow, orange, and finally, red. However, the spectrum isn't strictly limited to these colours. Intensity, or the amount of light, also affects perception, allowing humans to discern a multitude of shades and tints.

Calculating Light Colours

Understanding and calculating light colours require clear knowledge of the additive colour model. This model postulates that all colours result from varying combinations of red, green, and blue light, often noted as RGB. Colour calculations for digital media utilise this model, converting percentages of RGB values into hexadecimal codes. For instance, full intensity red would be calculated as (100%, 0%, 0%) in the RGB model and represented as FF0000 in hexadecimal coding.

The mathematical relation between the wavelength of light and its perceived colour is given by Planck's law of

Black-Body radiation. According to it, the colour of light with wavelength λ(in metres) at temperature T(in Kelvin) can be calculated using the formula:

$$\text{Intensity} \propto 2hc^2/\lambda^5 \times 1/(e^{(hc/\lambda kT)}-1)$$

Where h is Planck's constant; c is speed of light; and k is Boltzmann's constant.

Light and Quantum Mechanics

Light, with its wave-particle duality, plays a significant role in quantum mechanics. Physicists often utilise quantum mechanics' mathematical calculations to explore light's behaviour, revealing tremendous possibilities for various applications including quantum computing, encryption, and teleportation.

Light's wave-particle duality is a principle in quantum mechanics in which particles such as photons exhibit both particle and wave characteristics. This dual behaviour can only be understood using quantum mechanics, a field that explains the behavior of particles at the microscopic level. Albert Einstein, in his Nobel Prize-winning photoelectric effect explanation, proposed light might contain particles or "quanta", known as photons. Simultaneously, experiments such as Young's Double-Slit showcased light's wave-like characteristics such as interference and diffraction.

Light follows the quantum state behaviour demonstrated by Schrodinger's equation, a primary mathematical formula in quantum mechanics. This equation describes quantum systems evolution, relating system energy to wave function, a mathematical representation of the quantum state. Light's quantum state is usually expressed through the field's quantum harmonic oscillator solutions. The states, known as Fock states, describe a light system with definite photon numbers.

Mathematical formalism in quantum mechanics, including operators, vectors, and matrices' use, provides tools for calculating light behaviour. The creation operator, denoted as a , adds a photon to a quantum state, while the annihilation operator, represented as a, removes one photon. These operators, along with the commutation relations, contribute to solving quantum systems, including behaviours of light waves and particles.

Accurate mathematical calculations of light and its quantum mechanics have expanded the horizons of technology, particularly in areas such as quantum computing and cryptography. Quantum computing utilises quantum bits or 'qubits,' sometimes represented using the quantum state of photons. Quantum encryption, on the other hand, employs photons' quantum state to establish secure communication channels, using techniques such as quantum key distribution.

Photonics and Optoelectronics

The science of photonics, originating from the Greek word "photos" meaning light, was coined in the 1960s after the invention of the laser. It involves the generation, emission, transmission, modulation, signal processing, switching, amplification, and detection of light. Photonics finds application in a wide range of areas including communications, information processing, lighting, manufacturing, microscopy, and healthcare.

Within photonics, we find a major subset known as optoelectronics. This field combines physics, material science, and electronics to create applications such as laser systems, fibre optic communications, and solar photovoltaic panels. Optoelectronics is instrumental in the development of devices that emit, manipulate, and detect light.

Photonics and optoelectronics have crucial roles in several technological advancements. Communication systems, for instance, have transformed over the past few decades mainly due to advancements in photonic technologies, such as the application of optical fibre technology for high-speed data transmission. The roll-out of broadband network services has been greatly facilitated by optoelectronic technologies that allow for the exchange of a large amount of data at high speeds.

Solar energy utilisation has also seen significant improvements with the adoption of photovoltaic technology. This innovative technology uses semiconductor materials to convert sunlight into electric energy. Advancements in optoelectronics research have led to the development of more efficient and cheaper photovoltaic cells, making solar power a feasible and increasingly popular renewable energy source.

Optoelectronic devices like LEDs (Light Emitting Diodes) and OLEDs (Organic Light Emitting Diodes) have revolutionised lighting systems. They offer the advantages of small size, longer life, high reliability, low power consumption, and environmental friendliness. LEDs and OLEDs are now ubiquitous in displays, from mobile devices to large-scale screens and high definition televisions.

Light Speed and Special Relativity

The understanding of physics was indelibly modified by Albert Einstein's Special Theory of Relativity, inextricably binding the concepts of time, space, and, most significantly, light's speed. Light Speed and Special Relativity are integral elements of modern physics due to their fundamental role in shaping our comprehension of the Universe. The paper illuminates the mathematical implications of light speed in relation to Einstein's Theory of Special Relativity, underscoring the consequential landscapes of the physical world.

At its core is the revolutionary idea that the velocity of light in a vacuum (c) remains constant irrespective of the observer's motion or the source of light. This velocity is approximately 299,792 km/s, a universal constant denoted by 'c' in equations.

Einstein's work is based on two key postulates. The first asserts the principle of relativity, maintaining that the laws of physics are identical in all inertial frames. The second postulate contends that light's speed in vacuum is constant for all observers, irrespective of their state of motion or light source. These postulates, notably the latter, had revolutionary implications for the concept of time and space.

One profound implication of these postulates is the concept of time dilation. The formula is mathematically represented as $T = To / \sqrt{(1 - v^2/c^2)}$, where T is the dilated time, To is the stationary time, and v is the speed of the object relative to the stationary observer. As an object's speed edges closer to the speed of light, the factor $1/\sqrt{(1 - v^2/c^2)}$, colloquially known as gamma, exponentially increases, causing time to dilate or slow down towards an infinitely large value.

Simultaneously, the Special Theory of Relativity introduces length contraction, an extraordinary phenomenon where the lengths of objects contract along the direction of motion as they approach light speed. The corresponding mathematical expression is $L = Lo \sqrt{(1 - v^2/c^2)}$, where L represents the contracted length and Lo denotes the proper length or the length of the stationary object. Similar to time dilation, gamma impacts length contraction, causing objects to become infinitely short as they near the speed of light.

Einstein's energy-mass equation, $E=mc^2$, foregrounds another pivotal concept in special relativity. It encapsulates the profound truth that energy (E) and mass (m) are interchangeable entities related via light's speed (c) squared, yielding ground breaking implications for nuclear energy development.

Concepts of Fluid Mechanics

Fluid mechanics is a substantive branch of physics concerned with the behaviour of liquids and gases in rest or motion. It is a sub-discipline of continuum mechanics, the study of physical phenomena of continuous materials. As such, fluid mechanics is wide-ranging.

Two primary subdivisions classify the field of fluid mechanics: fluid statics or hydrostatics, which engages the physics of fluid at rest, and fluid dynamics, studying fluids in motion. Fluid statics investigates how forces balance across fluid interfaces, particularly for gases and liquids at rest under the effects of gravity and other forces. Practical applications of fluid statics include the design of dams, fuel tanks, swimming pools, and systems concerning atmospheric pressure.

On the other hand, fluid dynamics considers the details of flow velocity, pressure, density, and temperature as functions of space and time. Patterns of flow formation, wave anticipation, and related phenomena fall under this broad subdivision. It further divides into hydrodynamics (for liquids) and aerodynamics (for gases). Applications range from predicting and controlling the flow around aircraft and automobiles to designing pumps and turbines.

The principles of fluid mechanics are resolutely rooted in laws of nature such as conservation laws of mass ("Continuity Equation"), momentum (Newton's Second

Law), and energy. In addition, an understanding of force balance is mandatory to describe the behaviour of fluids. Fluid mechanics incorporates these principles into a set of governing equations that can describe the fluid's behaviour under various physical situations.

Furthermore, the study of fluid mechanics incorporates both empirical and theoretical analysis, with various degrees of idealisation. The method of idealisation, based on simplifications of reality, eases the process of understanding the complex flow phenomena. Ideal fluids are non-viscous (zero viscosity) and incompressible, leading to significant simplifications in deriving solutions for flow patterns.

Properties of Fluids

The four fundamental properties of fluids are density, viscosity, pressure, and temperature.

Density, signified as ρ, is an essential property of fluid. It is defined as mass contained per unit volume of a substance. The density of any fluid ultimately influences its buoyancy. For instance, an object will float in a fluid if its density is less than the fluid's density. The unit of density in the International System of Units (SI) is kilogram per cubic metre (kg/m^3).

Viscosity is another key property that shows a fluid's resistance to flow. Viscous fluids, like honey, resist flow more than less viscous fluids like water. It is this quality of the fluid which makes objects encounter resistance while moving through it, an aspect known as drag. Viscosity is often associated with the thickness of the fluid, and the SI unit is the Pascal-second (Pa.s).

Next, pressure, denoted as P, is one of the consequential properties of fluids. It is the force exerted by the fluid per unit area. This force is always directed at right angles to the surface it contacts, a phenomenon that explains why fluid pressure can be felt in all directions. The unit of pressure in SI is Pascal (Pa).

Lastly, temperature is a property that measures the thermal state of a fluid. The temperature of a fluid exerts a notable impact on both its density and viscosity. High temperatures generally lower the density and viscosity of most fluids. The SI unit for temperature is Kelvin (K).

Pressure and Buoyancy

Pressure, in fluid mechanics, refers to the perpendicular force exerted by fluid per unit area. It is expressed in units of force per unit area, such as Pascals (Pa), where 1 Pascal equals 1 Newton per square metre. Importantly, fluid pressure is isotropic, meaning it acts equally in all directions at any given point within the fluid.

Key variables influencing fluid pressure are altitude or depth within the fluid, the fluid's density, acceleration due to gravity, and any external pressure applied. The first three variables make up the equation $P = \rho g h$, known as the hydrostatic pressure equation, where P is the absolute pressure, ρ is fluid density, g is acceleration due to gravity, and h is the fluid's height or depth.

Buoyancy, the principle defined by Archimedes, is the upward force exerted by a fluid that opposes the weight of an immersed object. In simple terms, this force is what makes an object float or sink when immersed or partly submerged in a fluid.

The magnitude of buoyancy is determined by the volume of fluid displaced by the immersed object, the fluid's density and the local acceleration due to gravity. Mathematically, this is expressed as $F = \rho V g$, where F is the buoyant force, ρ is fluid density (of displaced fluid), V is the immersed object's volume, and g is the acceleration due to gravity.

The relationship between pressure and buoyancy cannot be understated. Pressure differences around an immersed object cause the buoyant force. The pressure is greater at the bottom than at the top of an object submerged in a fluid due to the fluid's weight above the deeper part. This pressure difference results in the upward buoyant force.

Understanding the concepts of pressure and buoyancy is a critical foundation for the discipline of fluid mechanics. Their impact extends beyond the world of academia, with practical implications in many industries, including engineering, environmental studies, and even medical and health studies. Hence, thorough knowledge in these areas forms the basis for many innovative technological solutions.

A multitude of experiments can be designed to demonstrate these principles, imparting a practical understanding of these concepts. Therefore, a precise interpretation of pressure and buoyancy in fluid mechanics serves as a basis for new research and study, thus, continually improving and innovating technological advancement throughout various sectors.

To sum up, the fluid mechanics principles of pressure and buoyancy are invaluable across several scientific fronts. The implications of these concepts and their in-depth understanding form a pivotal part of the scientific community. The study of pressure and buoyancy aids in crafting new methodologies, thereby pushing the boundaries of technological advancement forward.

Dynamics of Particle Physics

Particle physics, also known as High Energy Physics (HEP), is a branch of physics that studies the nature of particles that constitute matter and radiation. An understanding of particle physics is crucial to understanding the universe's fundamental constituents and forces. Simultaneously, mathematics plays a pivotal role in the theoretical derivation and practical application of particle physics concepts.

Fundamentals of Particle Physics

The standard model is an integral part of particle physics, offering a wide spectrum of understanding regarding subatomic particles' classifications and interactions. This model categorises elementary particles into Fermions (matter particles) and Bosons (force particles). Fermions include Quarks and Leptons, while the Bosons category involves Gauge Bosons (responsible for force transmission) and Higgs Boson; responsible for imparting particles with their respective masses.

Mathematically, the properties and behaviours of elementary particles are governed by quantum mechanics (QM) and quantum field theory (QFT). Schroedinger's wave equation, the cornerstone of QM, describes the behaviour and position of a particle in terms of probabilities rather than exact measures.

$$\Psi' + [2m / \hbar^2 * (E - V) - \Psi] = 0.$$

Where Ψ represents the wavefunction of the particle, m stands for the particle's mass, E signifies energy, V illustrates the particle's potential energy, and $\hbar$ indicates the reduced Planck's constant.

In QFT, particles are envisioned as excitations in a 'field,' with their behaviour explained through specific equations named Lagrangians. The simplest quantum field, the free scalar field, obeys the Klein-Gordon equation:

$$\partial\mu\partial\mu\phi + m^2\phi = 0$$

This equation represents a fundamental scalar boson of mass m, where ϕ represents the field, and the term $\partial\mu\partial\mu\phi$ implies the four-dimensional Laplacian of the field ϕ.

Particle physics engages in identifying the forces controlling particle behaviour. Four fundamental forces of nature - gravitational, electromagnetic, weak nuclear, and strong nuclear force - are vital in this pursuit. Each with specific properties, these forces are mathematically presented using quantum mechanics and field theories, such as Quantum ElectroDynamics (QED), Quantum ChromoDynamics (QCD), and the electroweak theory.

The Feynman diagrams provide a simplified graphical representation of the interactions between particles in relation to these forces. These diagrams depict the particles as lines and their interactions as vertices, thus visually demonstrating complex calculations.

Though particle physics has enjoyed substantial development, the model cannot clarify the mystery of 'dark matter', or unify gravity with other fundamental forces. This has led to the exploration of new theories like supersymmetry, string theory, and quantum gravity. While physics moves towards a 'Theory of Everything', the mathematical constructs behind particle physics will remain fundamental.

Particle Interactions and Interchange

Particle interactions, also known as fundamental forces or fundamental interactions, are the processes whereby particles interact with each other. They are the matrix serving as the groundwork for the dynamism and activity witnessed within the universe. There are four well-accepted types of particle interactions: gravitational, electromagnetic, weak nuclear, and strong nuclear forces.

Gravity is the most identifiable and ubiquitously experienced force. It manifests between any two masses in the universe and is responsible for the macro-structure of the universe, including planets revolving around stars. Conversely, electromagnetic forces involve the interaction between charged particles. This interaction forms the basis for chemistry and the grand scheme of life itself.

The weak nuclear force, on the other hand, is a critical component of many nuclear processes, such as radioactive decay. Unlike gravity, it acts only over minute distances and is responsible for certain types of particle decay. Lastly, the strong nuclear force binds protons and neutrons together in the atomic nuclei. Its name corresponds to its extraordinary strength, 100 times stronger than the electromagnetic force.

Particle interchange refers to situations where particles transform or convert into one another. Particle interchange is most noticeable in the realms of particle and high-energy physics. One prime example is beta decay, where a neutron converts into a proton by emitting a $W-$ boson that further decays into an electron and an electron antineutrino.

The study of such transformations has facilitated advancements in understanding the universe's nature. Specifically, it has heralded the development of the Standard Model, a theory in particle physics that describes the electromagnetic, weak, and strong nuclear interactions. This model has accurately described the behaviour of all known elementary particles, with the heavy Higgs boson discovery in 2012 providing the capstone evidence.

Quantum Field Theory and the Standard Model

In essence, QFT is the framework used to construct physical models of subatomic particle behaviour in quantum mechanics. Rather than considering particles as discrete entities, they are seen as excited states of the underlying physical field. This concept elegantly unifies both quantum theory and special relativity.

Fields exist throughout the universe, and they represent a value for a particular quantity that varies depending on location and time variables. Notably, quantum fields enable us to describe and interpret phenomena that cannot be satisfactorily explained by classical physics alone due to their quantum variables, such as particle entanglement and Heisenberg's uncertainty principle.

Particles, in the lens of QFT, are perturbations or 'quanta' in a particular field, with each particle type corresponding to its specific quantum field. The behaviour and advancement of these excitations are governed by quantum mechanics, falling in line with the probabilistic nature of the field.

The Standard Model

The Standard Model is one of the most successful models in modern physics, articulating the properties as well as interactions between elementary particles. It describes matter as being composed of two fundamental types of entities: particles of matter known as fermions and force-carrying particles known as bosons.

In the Standard Model, QFT acts as the perfect scaffold, laying down a structured framework of how particles interact. For instance, the electromagnetic force between two electrons can be depicted as an exchange of virtual photons, the quanta of the electromagnetic field, reflecting QFT's notion of fields and excitations.

Collision events in particle accelerators, the peculiar behaviours of quarks, the unification of electromagnetic and weak nuclear forces - all these are addressed and explained with profound elegance and precision by the Standard Model, with QFT providing the fundamental theoretical framework.

Laws of Photonics

Photonics evolved from optics, a branch of physics focusing on the behaviour and properties of light. Optics also includes the interaction of light with matter and the construction of instruments that use or detect light. However, photonics includes the quantum mechanical properties of light. In photonics, physicists and engineers take advantage of the particle nature of light, embodied in photons, to achieve new technologies and methodologies that have been producing groundbreaking contraptions in various fields.

Photonics is critical in a multitude of application areas, from healthcare to defence, telecommunications, computing, and much more. For example, in medicine, photonics technologies have brought breakthroughs in detecting, diagnosing, and treating diseases. In telecommunications, they're paving the way for fibre-optic communication, which can carry exponentially more data over long distances than traditional copper cables. Industries like manufacturing and energy are being revolutionised by photonics via advanced laser technology and solar energy applications, respectively.

The laws of photonics, given its roots in optics, adhere to the principles of optics and quantum mechanics. These involve reflection, refraction, diffraction, interference, polarisation, and the dual nature of light. Light reflection follows the law of reflection, stating the angle of incidence equals the angle of reflection. Refraction, measured by Snell's Law, describes how light changes direction when moving from one medium to another of different densities.

Diffraction is the bending of waves around obstacles, while interference involves the superposition of two or more waves that results in a new wave pattern. Light polarisation, dictated by Malus's Law, deals with the orientation of oscillations in the light wave. Lastly, the dual nature of light, which Einstein established in his photoelectric effect, reveals that light acts both as a particle and a wave.

Another key law in photonics is Planck's Law, which defines the spectrum of black-body radiation, a basis for describing light's interaction with matter. According to this law, the energy of a photon is directly proportional to its frequency, demonstrating the quantum nature of light.

Besides these primary laws, other principles and equations are integral to photonics, such as Maxwell's equations, the wave-particle duality, and quantum entanglement.

Electromagnetic Radiation and Interference

Electromagnetic radiation (EMR) is energy that traverses through space or matter. This encompasses a broad range of phenomena, including gamma rays, X-rays, ultraviolet radiation, visible light, radio waves, and microwaves. EMR is a fundamental aspect of the physical world, responsible for numerous natural phenomena and essential for several domains, such as telecommunications and medicine.

Any device that emits electromagnetic energy such as radios, televisions, cordless phones, Wi-Fi, and Bluetooth devices, can be a source of electromagnetic radiation. Another inherent aspect of EMR is the potential for electromagnetic interference (EMI), a disturbance caused by an external source affecting an electrical circuit. These disturbances may interrupt, obstruct, degrade, or limit the effective performance of the circuit.

EMI can be grouped into two categories: Narrowband and Broadband. Narrowband interference is generated by transmitters, devices, or equipment operating at a specific frequency. Examples include radios and televisions. Broadband interference, on the other hand, spans a wide range of frequencies and is often caused by devices like electric motors or fluorescent lights.

EMI often occurs due to lack of sufficient shielding or incorrect configuration and can cause significant issues for electronic devices. For example, EMI can disrupt the operation of critical medical devices in hospitals or interfere with navigation systems in aircraft. Hence, it is essential to understand and mitigate EMI to ensure the smooth functioning of electronic devices.

The mitigation of electromagnetic interference involves certain strategies. These include effective circuit layout and design, using shielded cables and connectors, employing filters to eliminate unwanted signals, isolating susceptible components and interconnecting layouts, ensuring good grounding techniques, and following industry best practices for EMI prevention.

In this digital age, electromagnetic interference takes on an increased significance. As the number of electronic devices and systems grows exponentially, the potential for interference rises correspondingly. Therefore, it is of utmost importance that electronic products undergo conformity assessment procedures to ensure they comply with international standards and norms on electromagnetic interference.

Applications of Photonics in Science and Technology

Photonics is the science of light and its applications, particularly involving the creation, detection, and manipulation of photons. This field has numerous applications across various sectors in science and technology, capable of revolutionising processes and enhancing existing technologies.

In computing, photonic technology is becoming increasingly important. Optical computers, which use light instead of electricity, are at the frontier of future computer technologies. Photonic microprocessors are much faster and use less power than electronic ones. They can also handle a vast amount of data quickly, which is essential in our data-driven world.

Telecommunications extensively utilise photonic technology, particularly in fibre optic communication systems. Here, light passes through optical fibres at high speed, carrying information. This technology allows for the fast, reliable, and high-capacity transmission of data over long distances. Moreover, photonic signal processing, which manipulates the information that light waves carry, enhances data transmission efficiency through coding and modulation.

In healthcare, biomedical photonics bring numerous innovations. Confocal microscopes use lasers to generate detailed 3D cell images, providing valuable insights into diseases like cancer. Photodynamic therapy employs photosensitive drugs and light to kill cancer cells, demonstrating the potential of photonics in novel treatments.

Furthermore, photonics offers novel methods for non-invasive measurements in medicine. Optical imaging tools, including optical coherence tomography and photoacoustic imaging, can visualise the human body's internal structures in high resolution and real-time.

In energy production, photonic technologies are vital in solar energy harvesting. Photovoltaic cells, in which photons from sunlight knock electrons loose, generate electricity. Improvements in photonic designs have significantly increased the efficiency of these cells, making solar power a more viable alternative to fossil fuels.

Photonics is crucial in environmental science. Many monitoring systems utilise photonics for air and water quality assessment, studying atmospheric composition, detecting pollutants, and monitoring ocean health. Lidar technology, which uses light to measure distances, generates precise 3D maps for environmental evaluation.

In manufacturing and materials science, photonics-based technologies like laser machining, 3D printing, and optical metrology offer precision, speed, and capabilities beyond traditional methods. Photonics excels at processing materials at a microscopic level, enabling the creation of devices with features on the nanoscale.

Concepts of Relativity

The world of physics was fundamentally transformed in the early 20th century by Albert Einstein's theories of relativity: the special theory of relativity and the general theory of relativity. These theories introduced radically new concepts to our understanding of the natural and physical world, upending established norms in Newtonian physics.

Special relativity theory primarily concerns the relationship between space and time. It postulates that the laws of physics are the same for all observers, regardless of their state of motion or non-motion. Furthermore, it states that the speed of light in a vacuum is constant, regardless of the motion state of the light source or observer. These postulates lead to strange and seemingly paradoxical phenomena such as time dilation and length contraction.

Time dilation and length contraction are direct consequences of the constancy of the speed of light. Time dilation refers to the phenomenon where time passes at different rates in regions of differing gravity or velocity. An observer in a high gravity or high-speed environment will experience time as passing more slowly compared to someone in a lower gravity or lower speed environment. Conversely, length contraction refers to the phenomenon where an object's length, as observed from a moving frame of reference, decreases as its speed relative to the observer increases.

General relativity theory (GR), developed a decade after SR, is a theory of gravitation. It extends SR by including acceleration and gravity into its framework. GR postulates that gravity is not a force exerted in space, but a manifestation of space-time curvature caused by mass and energy. More massive objects cause more extensive deformation of the space-time fabric, which we perceive as a stronger gravitational pull.

The most celebrated prediction of GR, the bending of light by gravity, was confirmed during a solar eclipse in 1919. Moreover, GR predicted the existence of black holes, regions of space-time with extreme gravity from which nothing, not even light, can escape. The first direct observation of a black hole in 2019 validated this prediction.

Einstein's theories of relativity have revolutionised our understanding of the universe. They have not only shaped our comprehension of the cosmos but also found pragmatic application. Technologies such as the Global Positioning System (GPS) rely on principles derived from SR and GR for their operation and accuracy.

Atomic Physics

The nucleus and electrons within an atom are bound together by two of the four fundamental forces in physics. The gravitational and weak nuclear forces have negligible effects at the atomic scale, leaving only the electromagnetic force and the strong nuclear force to sustain atoms' stability. Examining these forces in intricate detail is a critical facet of atomic physics.

The principal concern of atomic physics revolves around understanding and predicting how electrons interact with the powerful electromagnetic force. Surrounded by a field, electrons occupy energy levels around the nucleus. These levels, or shells, are calculated via quantum physics, giving rise to the concept of quantum numbers and electron configuration.

The Bohr model, established in 1913 by Danish physicist Niels Bohr, was the first to provide an accurate explanation of electron behaviour and was indeed a significant breakthrough in atomic physics. His atomic theory, based on quantum theory, described atoms as small solar systems with electrons orbiting the nucleus, just like planets around a sun.

Despite the relative simplicity of Bohr's model, the complexities of atomic interactions demanded far more sophisticated models to accurately describe the atomic environment. Quantum mechanics played a vital role in advancing atomic physics. The theory of quantum mechanics brought forth the concept of wave-particle duality, positively affecting the interpretations of atomic and subatomic phenomena.

A remarkable discovery in atomic physics is the principles of quantum superposition and entanglement. Superposition considers that particles exist in many states simultaneously, only committing to one when observed or measured. On the other hand, quantum entanglement demonstrates that particles can become interconnected, such that the status of one instantaneously influences another, regardless of the distance.

Nature of Time and Space

The Big Bang Theory

The Big Bang Theory represents one of the most significant theories in cosmology and physics, offering an explanation for the origin of the universe.

Like many theories in astrophysics and cosmology, the Big Bang Theory emanates from Albert Einstein's prodigious work in relativity, particularly his field equations. Einstein's field equation is a set of ten interrelated differential equations. These equations, which define the fundamental interaction between matter-energy and spacetime, form the basis of Einstein's general theory of relativity and are central to the Big Bang Theory.

These equations depict how matter and energy affect the curvature of spacetime, which subsequently influences the movement of matter and energy within spacetime. Therefore, the equations provide a mathematical framework embodying a possible manifestation of the universe. They contribute significantly to the mathematical representation of the Big Bang Theory.

These complex differential equations' solutions give rise to what cosmologists term 'models of the universe.' One such model, proposed by Alexander Friedmann in 1922, informed the inception of the hot Big Bang Theory. The expanding model of the universe hypothesised by Friedmann fits the prevalent understanding that the universe is in a constant state of expansion.

Issuing from Einstein's equations, the Friedmann equations encapsulate the universe's expansion dynamics. The equations propose that the universe's rate of expansion is directly proportional to the amount of matter and energy present. When these equations are combined with observations of distant galaxies, most notably, Edwin Hubble's work, scientists indeed corroborated that the universe is expanding. Thus, it is the application of mathematical principles through these equations that led to the general affirmation of the Big Bang Theory.

Further, the Big Bang Theory suggests that spacetime originated from a singularity, a point of infinite density and temperature. To explain such a phenomenon demands delving into the realm of Quantum Mechanics and thus leads to the fusion of Quantum Mechanics and Relativity. This fusion gives rise to Quantum Gravity, a theory often used to discuss the initial singularity from which the universe likely originated. The mathematics of Quantum Gravity is presently conjectural, operating at the cutting-edge of theoretical physics and cosmology.

III

High-Performance Computing and Advanced Algorithms

High-Performance Computing (HPC) essentially refers to aggregated computing power to deliver significantly higher performance than typical desktop computers and thus are capable of solving complex computational problems. HPC systems function effectively by dividing complex tasks into smaller parts that work simultaneously using interconnected networks. Algorithms govern this division and decision-making process in HPC systems.

Parallel Computing

High-Performance Computing (HPC) has increasingly become a crucial technology worldwide due to its profound capabilities in manipulating onerous datasets and managing sophisticated algorithms. Predominantly, HPC facilitates sophisticated computational simulations, data analysis, and predictive modelling, primarily increasing productivity, speeding up discoveries, and enhancing decision-making processes. The technology plays a crucial role in various fields including scientific research, financial services, medicine, and petrochemical industries. Central to HPC's enhanced computational efficiency is the concept of parallel computing.

Parallel computing, an area of computer science, allows several calculations or processes to run simultaneously. As an HPC approach, parallel computing plays a critical role in harnessing the full power of modern computers, making it a crucial component in the realm of advanced algorithms. This article delves into high-performance computing and advanced algorithms, mainly focussing on the significance of parallel computing.

It dispenses with the traditional, linear approach to computation, where each process executes independently and without an overlap in time. Instead, it separates complex computations into smaller concurrent tasks, significantly reducing the time taken to solve complex problems. By splitting a larger problem into smaller interconnected parts, it resembles the divide-and-conquer tactic, thereby boosting computational efficiency and speed, culminating in higher performance.

The architecture in parallel computing significantly improves speed and performance in computational tasks-an improvement essential for the demands of modern data volumes and complexities that require exceptionally fast processing speeds. In parallel computing, data splits into smaller packages, ensuring a swift concurrent processing that drastically reduces the overall computational time. Mainstream parallel computing architectures include the shared-memory architecture and the distributed system.

Parallel computing utilises advanced algorithms to ensure successful data processing. An algorithm in computer science is a series of steps used to solve computational problems. These algorithms are often complex and require high-performance computational strength for effective operation. And that is where HPC and parallel computing come in.

However, implementing and managing parallel computing can be somewhat challenging due to its complexity. It requires careful planning and coordinating the simultaneous execution of tasks without conflict. Nevertheless, the benefits greatly outweigh the challenges. Therefore, continuous research is being conducted to improve the way algorithms and software are devised for better optimization of parallel computing.

It is essential to note that parallel computing and HPC applications have wide-ranging implications in a variety of sectors. In healthcare, they can decipher complex genomic sequences and develop more effective drugs. Financial institutions rely on HPC to simulate economic models, forecast market trends, and manage risks. The automotive industry utilises HPC to design vehicles, simulate crash tests, and optimise fuel efficiency. Additionally, in meteorology, HPC facilitates the forecast of weather patterns and the prediction of disastrous climatic conditions.

High-performance computing and advanced algorithms have significantly changed the landscape of data processing. Parallel computing, central to this transformation, has streamlined efficiency and effectiveness in solving computational problems. As technology continually evolves, so does the need for more advanced and efficient computational algorithms. As such, researchers and engineers must continue to devise more sophisticated and efficient algorithms to keep up with technology's pace.

Grid Computing

Grid computing offers a multi-site infrastructure sharing model, allowing users to share computing power, data, and other resources transparently across dispersed departments, organisations, and geographical locations. This approach advertently overcomes the limitations of traditional standalone systems, presenting reliable and affordable solutions to industries repeatedly confronting colossal data challenges.

In grid computing, every computer on the network can work independently of others. This contrasts starkly to the concept of a traditional computer cluster, wherein networked computers need to perform identical tasks and are controlled and scheduled by centralised software. Because each grid computer can operate separately from the others, diversity is welcomed; machines can be running different operating systems and can be located anywhere globally, resulting in its heterogeneous environment.

Moreover, grid computing's fault tolerance is praiseworthy. If one computer in the network crashes, the system continues to function effectively with the available computers, ensuring operational continuity and no downtime.

The potential applications for grid computing are vast and range across numerous sectors. In the healthcare industry, it can help handle increasing volumes of medical data, enabling researchers to conduct comprehensive DNA analyses and complex medical imaging procedures. In the oil and gas industry, grid computing can be deployed for seismic interpretation and reservoir simulation to facilitate the discovery of new reserves and optimization of current reserves. It's a transformative way that grid computing makes an enormous impact on our everyday lives.

The application of grid computing in research settings is becoming increasingly common, owing to its ability to handle extensive data sets. Universities, research institutions, and organisations can greatly benefit from the immense computational power that grid computing provides, facilitating research and providing a platform for collaboration on a global scale.

However, several challenges impede the widespread adoption of grid computing. These include issues related to security, interoperability, software, and system administration complexities, and economic concerns. Achieving ease of use while maintaining security in a shared, publicly accessible, and often anonymous grid environment is a significant challenge. Further, ensuring smooth interoperability between numerous independent systems that come with their unique software and hardware configurations remains a daunting task.

Distributed Computing

The Roots of Distributed Computing

The origins of distributed computing date back to the 1970s, spurred by advances in computer technology. In the nascent stages, distributed computing was often referred to as resource-sharing computation. It allowed diverse computational resources from different geographical locations to be used to solve a large computing problem.

Distributed Computing Architectures

Distributed computing systems may be arranged in various architectural styles, including peer-to-peer networks and client-server architecture. The client-server architecture involves servers providing services while clients request and process them. Conversely, peer-to-peer networks consider all nodes equally, allowing each to act as both a server and a client.

Fundamental Concepts in Distributed Computing

Distributed computing invokes several concepts, including concurrency of components, lack of a global clock, and independent failures of components. Concurrency denotes simultaneous execution of multiple interacting computational tasks. Lack of a global clock implies differing interpretations of computed events across different components. Independent failures imply the isolated breakdown of system components that does not cause a collapse in the overall system.

Benefits and Challenges of Distributed Computing

Distributed computing comes with a myriad of benefits, such as resource sharing, enhance computation speed, and improved system reliability due to the redundancy of system components. However, it brings its share of challenges like coordination and communication difficulties among components, managing failures, and ensuring data consistency and security.

Applications of Distributed Computing

On the application axis, distributed computing has been embraced across several sectors, including e-commerce, finance, healthcare, and social networks. In e-commerce, distributed systems facilitate the storage of vast amounts of customer data across different geographical locations in an efficient and reliable manner. In finance, distributed ledgers, such as blockchain, have revolutionized financial transactions' transparency and security.

Future of Distributed Computing

Girded by the rapid technological advancements, the future of distributed computing will play a pivotal role in emerging fields such as cyber-physical systems, Internet of Things

(IoT), and edge computing. The successful implementation of these fields will hinge on advanced distributed systems capable of processing large-scale data, integrating different technologies, and ensuring real-time response and reliability.

Artificial Intelligence Algorithms

Artificial Intelligence (AI) has evolved as a revolutionary technology that influences diverse sectors, from health to gaming, finance to transportation, and more. At the heart of this technology lies the sophisticated algorithms that power the AI systems. This article aims to delve deeper into the intriguing world of AI Algorithms.

What exactly is an Artificial Intelligence algorithm?

An AI algorithm is a complex set of instructions designed to perform specific tasks, solve problems, and make predictions by using data input. These sets of instructions enable a machine to mimic human cognition, learn from its experiences, predict human preferences and make independent decisions. AI algorithms are integrated into a myriad of applications such as search engines, email filters, personal assistants like Siri and Alexa, facial recognition software, and so on.

Types of AI Algorithms

There is a broad spectrum of AI algorithms, each with its unique abilities. The most common ones are:

1. Supervised Learning: In this AI algorithm, a model is trained on a labelled dataset. Essentially, the algorithm uses a number of inputs and outputs to create a function that maps

the relationship between them. Examples include Linear regression, Logistic regression, and Support vector machines.

2. Unsupervised Learning: As opposed to supervised learning, the algorithm in this case is used to identify patterns in datasets that aren't labelled. It discovers the underlying structure of data, and it's used in clustering, association, and dimensionality reduction tasks. Examples include K-means clustering and Principal Component Analysis (PCA).

3. Reinforcement Learning: Reinforcement learning focuses on improving its decisions based on the reward-or-punishment mechanism. The algorithm learns by interacting with its environment, observing the results of the actions, and adjusting its behaviours accordingly. An application example is DeepMind's AlphaGo, which used reinforcement learning to defeat the world champion in the board game Go.

Impact of AI algorithms in Today's World

AI algorithms impact every industry and our daily lives, often without us even realising it. For instance, recommendation algorithms on Netflix or Amazon make suggestions based on our past decisions. Furthermore, financial firms use AI-based algorithms for risk assessment, fraud detection, and to predict market trends.

Healthcare is another field that benefits hugely from AI algorithms. AI diagnostic tools help doctors analyse a huge amount of patient data, leading to accurate and fast disease diagnosis.

In transportation, AI algorithms power the navigation systems in our cars and are the backbone of autonomous vehicles. In the field of education, AI assists personalised learning by understanding each student's strengths and weaknesses and providing customised tutoring.

Natural Language Processing Algorithms

Natural Language Processing (NLP) is a subfield of Artificial Intelligence that focuses on the interaction between computers and humans through natural language. Its primary aim is to ensure that computers understand, interpret, and manipulate human language to perform more personalised tasks. Algorithms play a pivotal role in the execution of NLP by enabling a computer to understand, analyse, and gain meaningful insights from human language data. Let's delve into the fascinating world of Natural Language Processing algorithms.

To understand NLP algorithms, first, we need to comprehend the concept of algorithms. In computer science, an algorithm is a set of instructions to follow to solve a problem or accomplish a task. Similarly, NLP algorithms are rules or methods that computers use to understand human language. NLP algorithms can analyse contexts, sentiment, semantics, syntax, and relationships within the text to provide accurate results.

One of the primary NLP algorithms is Syntactic Analysis. This algorithm deals with understanding the grammatical structure of sentences. It applies grammatical rules to group words into phrases, which help ascertain the role of each word in the sentence. Doing this helps the algorithm understand the relation between different words, thereby enabling the computer to understand the text's context better.

Another significant NLP algorithm is Semantic Analysis. It goes beyond the sentence structure to understand the meaning conveyed by the text. It focuses on the interpretation of words and phrases in the context of sentences and larger chunks of text to extract meaningful interpretations. The semantic analysis algorithm uses techniques like Word Sense Disambiguation (determining the correct meaning of a word based on context) and Named Entity Recognition (identifying people, places, and organisations within the text).

The Sentiment Analysis algorithm in NLP is a great tool that helps understand emotions, opinions, and attitudes expressed in the text. It analyses the language and tone of a text to extract subjective information, often used to gauge customer attitudes towards products, services, or brand reputation.

Lastly, the Discourse Analysis algorithm focuses on analysing larger chunks of text, including paragraphs and documents, to understand the text's overall context. This algorithm is mainly used for text comprehension and summarization, conversation modelling, and machine translation.

Establishing these algorithms in a computer system requires training data, which is a set of data used to teach the machine how to interpret human language. Some of the methods used in training NLP algorithms include Supervised Learning (the algorithm is trained on a predetermined set of examples), Unsupervised Learning (the algorithm learns from patterns in data), and Reinforcement Learning (the algorithm learns by interfacing with its environment).

With the current trend in digital revolution and AI, the future of NLP algorithms seems promising. With advancements in Machine Learning and Deep Learning, NLP algorithms are becoming more sophisticated, leading to higher efficiency and accuracy in tasks such as sentiment analysis, machine translation, and chatbot interaction.

Graph Theory Algorithms

Graph theory algorithms are used to analyse and solve problems related to network structures. They involve solving problems such as finding shortest paths between nodes, finding network components, and finding the most efficient way to route data between nodes. Graph theory algorithms are also used in data mining and machine learning for tasks such as clustering, pattern recognition, and data classification.

To assist with solving problems related to graph theory algorithms, there are many tools available. These include specialised software, online services, and programming languages. Specialised software includes programs such as Gephi and Cytoscape which are used to visualise networks. Online services provide access to pre-made algorithms and data structures that can be used for solving problems. Programming languages such as Python and C++ provide the necessary tools for creating algorithms from scratch.

It can be used for many applications, ranging from biological research to traffic management. In biology, algorithms are used to analyse gene networks and cellular pathways. In traffic management, algorithms can be used to optimise the flow of traffic on roads and highways. Graph theory algorithms are also used in social network analysis and computer vision.

Graph theory algorithms are powerful tools for solving complex problems related to networks and data structures. With the right tools and knowledge, these algorithms can be used to analyse and optimise many different systems.

Image Processing Algorithms

Image processing algorithms are sets of instructions used to modify digital images. They can be used to improve the quality of the image, add special effects, or change the format of the image. Image processing algorithms can be implemented in software, hardware, or a combination of both.

Types of Image Processing Algorithms

Image processing algorithms can be divided into two main categories: linear and non-linear algorithms. Linear algorithms are used to modify the brightness, contrast, and colour of an image. Non-linear algorithms are used to detect and isolate specific features in an image, such as edges, lines, and objects.

Image processing algorithms are used in a variety of applications, including medical imaging, facial recognition, surveillance systems, and industrial automation. Medical imaging algorithms are used to detect abnormalities in medical scans, such as tumours or other abnormalities. Facial recognition algorithms are used to identify an individual from an image or video. Surveillance systems use image processing algorithms to detect and track objects in an environment. Industrial automation algorithms are used to detect defects in manufactured parts or products.

The advantages of using image processing algorithms include the ability to manipulate and analyse large amounts of data quickly and accurately. They also enable us to extract useful information from digital images, such as patterns, features, and objects. The disadvantages include the complexity of algorithms and the need for large amounts of computing power and memory.

Network Security Algorithms

Network Security Algorithms are essential components of cyber defence systems. These sets of instructions serve to safeguard data integrity, confidentiality, and availability within network systems, ensuring secure communication between authenticated users.

One of the most common types of network security algorithms is symmetric encryption. Here, the same key is used for both encryption and decryption of the message. The primary advantage of symmetric encryption algorithms is their speed and computational efficiency. The notable examples are the Data Encryption Standard (DES), Advanced Encryption Standard (AES), and the Triple DES (3DES) algorithms. AES, in particular, is widely recognized for its strong security and has been adopted by the US government for classified information encryption.

Another popular category is asymmetric encryption or public-key cryptography. In this case, two different keys are used: one private and one public. The public key encrypts the data, and the corresponding private key decrypts it. Examples of asymmetric encryption algorithms include the Rivest-Shamir-Adleman (RSA), Diffie-Hellman, Elliptical Curve Cryptography (ECC), and the Digital Signature Algorithm (DSA). Asymmetric encryption offers various benefits including secure key distribution and non-repudiation, notwithstanding the downside of being more computationally intensive than symmetric encryption.

Hash functions constitute another class of network security algorithms. They are designed to take an input message and convert it into a fixed-length string of characters, which is typically a digest. Hash functions are used in various applications like checksums and digital signatures. The SHA (Secure Hash Algorithm) family, including SHA-1, SHA-256, and SHA-3, alongside the Message Digest (MD) family, constitute prominent examples of hash function algorithms.

Stepping beyond classical cryptography, newer approaches like quantum cryptography present a different dimension of network security. Leveraging principles of quantum physics, quantum key distribution (QKD) protocols can offer theoretical, unconditionally secure communication. Quantum-resistant algorithms are being developed to future-proof network security measures against the potential threats posed by quantum computers.

Despite the varying kinds of network security algorithms, they share the common objective of maintaining the integrity, confidentiality, and availability of data. The selection of an appropriate algorithm should be driven by specific network requirements which take into account factors such as encryption speed, key distribution technique, and anticipated threat landscape.

The significance of network security algorithms is evident. However, their effectiveness hinges on their proper implementation and continual maintenance. Therefore, a comprehensive understanding of these algorithms is not only beneficial but necessary for all involved in network security management.

IV

Machine Learning and AI for Pattern Recognition

In the realm of technology and innovation, the fields of machine learning and artificial intelligence have emerged as game-changers. As we strive to unravel the mysteries hidden within vast amounts of data, these powerful tools have proven themselves indispensable in unlocking patterns that were once invisible to the human eye. With their ability to recognize complex patterns and make informed predictions, machine learning and AI are revolutionising countless industries, from healthcare to finance and beyond.

Supervised Learning

In today's rapidly advancing technological era, where data is being generated at an unprecedented rate, the need for intelligent systems capable of recognizing patterns and extracting valuable insights has never been greater. This is where the power of machine learning and artificial intelligence (AI) comes into play. Among various approaches to pattern recognition, supervised learning stands out as a key technique that enables machines to learn from labelled examples and make accurate predictions or classifications. By harnessing the capabilities of supervised learning algorithms, we can unlock new realms of possibility in fields such as image recognition, speech processing, and even healthcare diagnostics.

One of the key advantages of supervised learning is its ability to handle both classification and regression tasks. In classification, the goal is to assign input samples to predefined categories or classes, while regression aims at predicting a continuous output variable. With the availability of large annotated datasets, supervised learning models have achieved impressive results in various domains such as image recognition, speech processing, natural language understanding, and fraud detection.

To overcome challenges like overfitting or underfitting that occur due to limited training data or noisy labels, practitioners often employ techniques like cross-validation or regularisation methods. Another exciting development in supervised learning is transfer learning, using pre-trained models on one task as a starting point for another related task. This approach enables developers to leverage existing knowledge and adapt it to different scenarios without starting from scratch.

To illustrate supervised learning, consider the task of recognizing handwritten digits. A model can be trained using a dataset composed of images of handwritten digits along with their corresponding labels (i.e., the actual digit represented by each image). By leveraging techniques such as decision trees or neural networks, the model learns patterns that discriminate between different digits. Subsequently, when presented with new unlabeled images, the trained model applies its acquired knowledge to predict the correct digit label for each image.

Another example could be email spam filtering. In this scenario, an algorithm is trained on a dataset containing both legitimate emails and spam emails that have been annotated accordingly. The supervised learning algorithm analyses various features extracted from each email (e.g., subject line, sender address) and learns patterns indicative of either spam or legitimate content. Therefore, when confronted with incoming emails without labels, the trained model can effectively classify them as either spam or non-spam based on its acquired understanding of distinguishing characteristics.

Unsupervised Learning

Unsupervised Learning encompasses various computational methods that facilitate the automatic discovery of inherent structures and relationships within unlabelled data points. These techniques strive to uncover meaningful representations, clusters, or hidden factors through iterative processes involving dimensionality reduction or clustering algorithms. With its ability to discern underlying patterns without explicit supervision, Unsupervised Learning offers unique advantages over its supervised counterpart by alleviating the need for costly and labour-intensive manual annotation.

By employing Machine Learning and AI for Pattern Recognition via Unsupervised Learning approaches, researchers can unlock a plethora of applications across diverse domains such as computer vision, natural language processing, anomaly detection, and recommendation systems. This paradigm empowers machines to autonomously learn from vast amounts of unlabeled data, enabling them to make informed decisions based on extracted patterns rather than predefined rules. As this field continues to evolve rapidly, further advancements in algorithm development and optimization hold great promise for unravelling complex patterns buried within increasingly large and high-dimensional datasets.

To illustrate this approach, consider an example from image processing. Suppose we have a vast collection of unlabeled images capturing various landscapes. By applying unsupervised learning algorithms such as clustering techniques (e.g., k-means or hierarchical clustering), the ML model can identify groups of visually similar images based on colour distributions, texture features, or other visual attributes. Consequently, the model could automatically group images depicting mountains together, separate them from those featuring beaches or forests, and potentially detect subcategories within these landscapes based on their composite elements.

Another application domain where unsupervised learning shines is natural language processing (NLP). Let's imagine a scenario where we possess a large corpus of unannotated text documents from different domains. Utilising unsupervised learning algorithms like topic modelling (e.g., Latent Dirichlet Allocation), ML models can uncover underlying themes or topics present within the textual data. As a result, the model could identify clusters of documents discussing similar subjects such as politics, sports, economics, etc.

Reinforcement Learning

Reinforcement learning combines elements of supervised and unsupervised learning with an additional reward-based feedback mechanism. In RL, an agent interacts with an environment, taking actions and receiving feedback in the form of rewards or penalties based on its decisions. The goal is to optimise the agent's behaviour by learning how to map states to actions that maximise cumulative rewards over time. This process typically involves exploring different actions during initial stages to gather information about the environment, followed by exploiting learned knowledge to make informed decisions.

The integration of reinforcement learning into machine learning and AI systems for pattern recognition brings several advantages. RL allows agents to learn from trial-and-error interactions without relying on predefined training data labels, which makes it suitable for domains where labelled data may be scarce or expensive to obtain. Additionally, RL can handle sequential decision-making problems with delayed consequences efficiently. By incorporating reinforcement learning techniques into pattern recognition algorithms, we can enhance system capabilities in various real-world applications such as robotics control, game playing strategies, autonomous driving systems, and natural language processing tasks.

One prominent technique within machine learning for pattern recognition is reinforcement learning. This approach involves an agent interacting with an environment, learning optimal actions through trial-and-error, and receiving positive or negative rewards based on its decisions. Reinforcement learning models are trained using algorithms that optimise long-term cumulative rewards, enabling them to uncover complex patterns within dynamic environments.

To illustrate the practical applications of reinforcement learning in pattern recognition, let us consider a couple of examples. In robotics, reinforcement learning can be leveraged to teach a robotic arm how to grasp objects efficiently by attempting different grasping strategies and receiving feedback on their success rates. Similarly, in natural language processing tasks such as sentiment analysis, reinforcement learning models can be employed to categorise text into positive or negative sentiment by iteratively adjusting their decision-making processes based on provided reward signals.

Overall, the fusion of machine learning and AI techniques with reinforcement learning methodologies holds immense potential for advancing pattern recognition capabilities across diverse domains. By allowing systems to autonomously learn and adapt through interactions with their environment, these approaches contribute to more efficient and accurate identification of patterns in complex data sets.

V

Quantum Computing and the Revolution of Computational Power

Quantum computing, a field that once existed only in the realm of theory and science fiction, has now become a reality that promises to revolutionise computational power. Unlike classical computers that rely on bits to represent information as zeros or ones, quantum computers leverage the mind-bending phenomena of quantum mechanics, such as superposition and entanglement, to process data exponentially faster.

History of Quantum Computing

At the forefront of technological advancements, quantum computing holds a potential that could reshape our understanding of computation. It all began with Richard Feynman's groundbreaking idea in 1982, when he proposed using quantum systems to perform complex calculations beyond the capabilities of classical computers. Since then, researchers have made significant strides in harnessing this phenomenon by manipulating qubits, the fundamental units of information in quantum computing. This has opened up a world of possibilities, offering computational power far superior to anything we have seen before. This sparked interest among researchers who began exploring ways to build practical quantum computers. Significant breakthroughs followed in the late 1990s and early 2000s when scientists successfully implemented basic algorithms using small-scale qubit systems. Since then, progress has been rapid, with advancements in qubit technologies such as superconducting circuits and trapped ions leading to the development of more sophisticated and robust quantum processors.

Quantum mechanics, a branch of physics that describes the behaviour of particles at the atomic and subatomic levels, provides a unique framework for information processing. Unlike classical computers that rely on binary bits representing either 0 or 1, quantum computers employ quantum bits, or qubits, which can exist in multiple states simultaneously due to a phenomenon known as superposition.

This ability to exist in multiple states allows quantum computers to perform calculations exponentially faster than their classical counterparts. By exploiting another concept called entanglement, where two or more qubits become highly correlated even when separated by vast distances, quantum computers can process vast amounts of information simultaneously. These remarkable features open up new possibilities for solving complex problems that are currently intractable for classical computers.

Principles of Quantum Computing

The Principles of Quantum Computing entail the fundamental tenets that underpin the operation and potential of quantum computers. It is a cutting-edge field of research that leverages principles from quantum mechanics to develop novel computational paradigms. These principles encompass several key aspects, including superposition, entanglement, and quantum gates.

Superposition is an inherent property of quantum systems that allows them to exist in multiple states simultaneously. Unlike classical bits, which can only be either 0 or 1, qubits (quantum bits) can be in a superposition of both states at once. This property enables exponentially large computational spaces and holds great promise for solving complex problems efficiently.

Entanglement is another crucial principle in quantum computing wherein the state of one qubit becomes correlated with the state of another, regardless of their spatial separation. This interconnection enables information transfer and manipulation between qubits without direct physical interaction, forming the basis for powerful parallel computations.

Quantum gates form the building blocks of quantum circuits and operations performed on qubits. Similar to classical logic gates like AND or XOR, these specialised gates manipulate qubit states according to specific rules defined by quantum mechanics. By combining various quantum gates, sophisticated computations can be carried out effectively on a quantum computer.

Potential Applications of Quantum Computing

Quantum computing, an emerging field at the nexus of physics and computer science, holds immense promise for revolutionising computational capabilities across various domains. The inherent principles of quantum mechanics that underpin this paradigm enable the development of novel algorithms and computational techniques, offering potential applications with unparalleled efficiency and efficacy. These advancements have the potential to transform fields such as cryptography, optimization problems, and drug discovery.

One notable application lies in the realm of cryptography. Quantum computers possess the ability to factor large numbers exponentially faster than classical computers through algorithms like Shor's algorithm. Consequently, these powerful machines could render current encryption methods obsolete, thereby necessitating the development of new cryptographic protocols resistant to quantum attacks. For instance, post-quantum cryptography schemes based on lattice-based or code-based cryptosystems are being explored to mitigate the vulnerabilities posed by quantum adversaries.

Another compelling domain where quantum computing can make significant strides is optimization. Many real-world challenges involve finding optimal solutions among a vast number of possibilities – a task often computationally intensive for conventional systems. Quantum annealing approaches such as those offered by D-Wave Systems can potentially provide efficient solutions for optimization problems like scheduling, portfolio management, or logistics planning. By exploiting quantum phenomena such as superposition and entanglement, these computers can explore a broader solution space more effectively than classical counterparts.

Furthermore, quantum computing has considerable potential in accelerating drug discovery processes. Pharmaceutical research involves extensive computational simulations to identify promising compounds or predict their behaviour in complex biological systems.

VI

Superposition and Entanglement

In the mind-boggling realm of quantum physics, two phenomena reign supreme, defying our classical understanding of reality: superposition and entanglement. These concepts challenge the very foundations of how we perceive physical systems, introducing a bizarre world where particles can exist in multiple states simultaneously and become mysteriously intertwined across vast distances.

Quantum Mechanics

Have you ever wondered how particles can exist in multiple states at the same time? Or how they can instantaneously communicate with each other regardless of distance? Welcome to the mesmerising world of quantum mechanics, where concepts like superposition and entanglement challenge our intuition about how the universe operates. Unlike classical physics, which describes objects in definite states, quantum mechanics introduces a new set of rules that govern the behaviour of particles on a tiny scale.

Superposition and entanglement are fundamental concepts in the framework of quantum mechanics, which is a theory that describes the behaviour of particles at the microscopic level. Superposition refers to the intriguing property exhibited by quantum systems, wherein they can exist simultaneously in multiple states or configurations. In other words, a particle can be in a state that is a combination of different possibilities, only collapsing into a definite state when observed or measured.

Entanglement, on the other hand, involves an intricate correlation between two or more particles such that their individual properties become interdependent and inseparable. When particles become entangled, their states become entwined with each other and any measurement made on one particle instantaneously affects the state of the other(s). This bizarre phenomenon challenges our classical intuition as it suggests non-local correlations that seemingly transcend traditional notions of space and time.

These phenomena are deeply rooted in the mathematical formalism of quantum mechanics and have been extensively studied and verified through experiments. Their understanding has revolutionised our comprehension of nature at its most fundamental level, leading to remarkable technological advancements such as quantum computing and cryptography. The complex interplay between superposition and entanglement continues to be an active area of research, capturing the imagination of physicists as they delve deeper into the intricacies of quantum phenomena.

Bell's Theorem

Bell's theorem, named after physicist John Bell, addresses an important question: Can the correlations observed between entangled particles be explained by classical physics? In other words, could there be some hidden variables underlying these quantum phenomena that we just haven't discovered yet? Bell's theorem mathematically proves that no local hidden variable theory can account for all observed experimental results. It demonstrates that entanglement leads to correlations between particles that cannot be explained by any classical explanation, highlighting the truly non-classical nature of quantum mechanics.

Superposition Principle

Superposition, within the context of quantum physics, refers to a fundamental principle that allows for the simultaneous existence of multiple states or conditions of a system. This principle posits that an entity can exist in a state that is effectively a combination or linear summation of two or more individual states, with each state contributing to the overall probability distribution. Mathematically, superposition is represented by a linear combination of basis states, and these combinations can be expressed as complex numbers.

The crux of the superposition principle lies in its ability to provide an elegant framework for describing phenomena at the microscopic scale. By accommodating multiple potential states simultaneously, it enables a comprehensive representation of quantum systems that exhibit wave-particle duality. Furthermore, this principle carries profound implications for computation and information processing as it forms the foundation for quantum computing algorithms such as Shor's algorithm and Grover's search algorithm. Overall, superposition fundamentally challenges our classical understanding by demonstrating that particles can exist in different states concurrently until measured or observed.

In conjunction with superposition, entanglement emerges as another intriguing phenomenon within quantum mechanics. Entanglement involves the interconnection between two or more particles such that their combined state cannot be independently described but rather necessitates considering their joint state as a whole.

Non-Locality

Non-locality refers specifically to this property exhibited by entangled particles where measurement outcomes on one particle instantaneously affect those on another particle irrespective of any physical intermediary or transmission delay. It suggests that information is transmitted beyond what we typically consider as local space-time boundaries, violating classical principles such as locality and causality.

Schrödinger's Cat

An illustrative thought experiment devised by physicist Erwin Schrödinger. In this scenario, a hypothetical cat is placed inside a box along with a radioactive substance that has a 50% chance of decaying within a certain time frame. According to quantum theory, until the box is opened and observed, the cat exists in a superposition of being both alive and dead simultaneously.

Furthermore, entanglement is another extraordinary concept in quantum mechanics closely related to superposition. It occurs when two or more particles become intertwined in such a way that their states are intrinsically linked regardless of their distance from each other. This means that any change applied to one particle will instantaneously affect the other(s), irrespective of physical proximity or time delay. The implications of entanglement are mind-boggling; it suggests that information can be transmitted faster than light and challenges our classical understanding of causality.

Heisenberg Uncertainty Principle

The Heisenberg uncertainty principle, named after physicist Werner Heisenberg, postulates an intrinsic limit on our ability to precisely measure certain pairs of complementary properties for a given particle. It asserts that there exists a trade-off between measuring position and momentum or any other pair of conjugate variables with high precision simultaneously. In other words, the more accurately we determine one property such as position, the less precisely we can know its corresponding conjugate variable like momentum, resulting in inherent uncertainty within quantum systems. This principle embodies the fundamental indeterminacy present at the quantum level and has far-reaching consequences for our understanding of physical measurements and predictions concerning subatomic entities.

VII

Theory and Practice: Bridging the Gap

Quantum computing, the revolutionary field of study that harnesses the principles of quantum mechanics to process information, has long been confined to the realm of theory and speculation. However, recent breakthroughs in experimental technologies have brought this tantalising concept closer to reality than ever before.

Quantum Programming and Software Development

Quantum computing has long been the holy grail of computing technology, promising unparalleled computational power and revolutionising fields such as cryptography, drug discovery, and optimization. However, despite its immense potential, the practical implementation of quantum computers remains a monumental challenge. Bridging this gap between theory and practice requires advancements in quantum programming and software development to effectively harness the capabilities of these elusive machines.

Quantum programming, an emerging field within computational science and engineering, pertains to the development of software applications that harness the principles of quantum mechanics. This paradigm shift in programming is driven by the realisation that quantum computing systems possess immense computational power and can potentially solve complex problems with unprecedented efficiency. The realm of quantum programming necessitates a departure from classical binary logic and embraces the concept of qubits, which are analogous to classical bits but can exist in superposition states. Consequently, software developers must grapple with the intricate task of crafting algorithms that exploit this unique attribute to perform operations in parallel. Furthermore, given the sensitivity of quantum systems to noise and decoherence, programmers face additional challenges in designing error-correcting codes to enhance the reliability of quantum computations.

Software development for quantum systems represents a cutting-edge frontier marked by a fusion of computer science, physics, and mathematics. Quantum programming languages such as Qiskit and Microsoft's Q# provide developers with tools to express complex quantum algorithms concisely while abstracting away some underlying hardware details. However, due to the nascent nature of this domain, further research is required to refine these languages and develop new ones that better cater to specific applications. Additionally, advancements in software verification techniques must be pursued to guarantee correctness and optimise performance in an environment where classical assumptions no longer hold true.

Programming Languages

There are several programming languages that have emerged for quantum programming, each with its unique features and capabilities. One such language is Q#, developed by Microsoft, which aims to provide a high-level programming environment for writing quantum algorithms. It offers various libraries and tools specifically designed for quantum computing tasks, making it easier for developers to explore the potential of this field.

Another popular language in the world of quantum programming is Python. Known for its simplicity and readability, Python has gained popularity due to its rich ecosystem of libraries like Pyquil and Cirq, which allow users to experiment with quantum computing on existing hardware platforms. Python's vast community support also makes it an attractive choice for beginners who want to join the quantum computing revolution.

In addition to Q# and Python, IBM's Qiskit stands out as another powerful language for quantum programming. Built on top of Python, Qiskit allows users to access real or simulated hardware through Quantum Experience as well as leverage various tools like Aer and Terra. With comprehensive documentation and a large user base, Qiskit continues to enhance the accessibility of quantum programming while fostering innovation in this rapidly evolving field.

These are just a few examples of the many exciting options available in the realm of quantum programming languages. As researchers and developers continue pushing boundaries in this domain, new languages may emerge with even more advanced capabilities tailored specifically for unlocking the full potential of future quantum computers.

Error Correction and Fault Tolerance

Quantum computing Theory and Practice: Error Correction and Fault Tolerance is a profound area of research within the realm of quantum computation. It seeks to address the inherent fragility of quantum systems, which are highly susceptible to errors caused by environmental disturbances and imperfect physical operations. In this context, error correction refers to the development of sophisticated techniques aimed at mitigating the detrimental impact of these errors on quantum information processing.

One fundamental challenge in error correction lies in preserving the delicate coherence between qubits: the basic units of quantum information. To achieve this, fault tolerance mechanisms are employed to ensure that computational tasks can be executed reliably even in the presence of errors. These mechanisms often involve encoding logical qubits into multiple physical qubits, thus enhancing their resilience against noise-induced errors. Moreover, fault tolerance also encompasses error detection strategies that enable identification and localization of errors during computations.

The theoretical framework underlying error correction and fault tolerance draws heavily from various mathematical disciplines such as coding theory and linear algebra. Concepts like stabiliser codes, entanglement distillation, and quantum error-correcting codes form the backbone of this paradigm. On a practical level, these concepts are implemented using diverse hardware platforms and experimental techniques. The advancement of error correction and fault tolerance plays a pivotal role in realising the full potential of quantum computing by establishing a robust foundation for reliable computation amidst unavoidable sources of noise and imperfection.

Hardware

The theoretical aspect of quantum computing hardware encompasses a diverse range of topics such as quantum gate design, error correction codes, and quantum algorithms. Researchers grapple with designing new gate structures that can reliably manipulate qubits, the basic units of information in a quantum computer, while simultaneously minimising noise and decoherence effects. Moreover, investigating error correction codes becomes paramount as they provide mechanisms to mitigate the detrimental impacts of environmental disturbances on fragile qubits.

On the practical front, developing efficient methods for implementing these theoretical concepts is crucial. Engineers strive to construct stable physical systems capable of hosting qubits through various platforms such as superconducting circuits or trapped ions. This includes optimising control mechanisms to accurately initialise, manipulate, and measure qubits with high fidelity. Additionally, researchers tackle challenges associated with scaling up these hardware architectures to accommodate larger numbers of qubits while maintaining coherence and reducing errors.

Quantum computing theory and practice in relation to hardware present an intellectually stimulating area where complex mathematical formalism intertwines with sophisticated experimental techniques.

Security Considerations

Security considerations in quantum computing encompass a broad spectrum of issues that arise due to the inherent differences between classical and quantum computational frameworks. Quantum algorithms possess immense power, enabling them to break traditional cryptographic protocols with relative ease. Consequently, it becomes imperative to develop novel cryptographic techniques that are resistant to attacks from quantum computers. Additionally, the secure transmission of data over quantum networks, which leverage entanglement and superposition for communication, necessitates the development of robust encryption schemes capable of protecting sensitive information from eavesdropping or tampering.

Furthermore, the advent of practical quantum computers raises concerns regarding post-quantum cryptography. As these machines become more powerful and accessible, they may render many existing cryptographic methods obsolete. Therefore, there is a pressing need for researchers to identify and develop new cryptographic primitives that can withstand attacks from both classical and quantum adversaries. Moreover, exploring alternative cryptographic approaches such as lattice-based cryptography or code-based cryptography will play a crucial role in establishing secure systems for future generations.

VIII

Virtual Experimentation and Calculation-Based Analyses

Virtual experimentation involves the application of computational techniques and simulation models to emulate real-world phenomena in a controlled digital environment. This emerging methodology leverages complex algorithms and mathematical equations to replicate the behaviour and interactions of objects, systems, or processes that would typically be studied through physical experiments.

Calculation-Based Analyses of Quantum Computing

These analyses utilise complex algorithms and mathematical models to evaluate various aspects of quantum computing, such as algorithmic efficiency, error correction techniques, and computational complexity.

For instance, one example of calculation-based analysis is the study of quantum algorithms like Shor's algorithm. This algorithm has sparked considerable interest as it can efficiently factor large numbers, a task that poses significant challenges for classical computers. By applying calculation-based analyses, researchers can investigate the theoretical underpinnings of Shor's algorithm, assess its performance in different scenarios, and explore potential modifications or improvements.

Another example is the evaluation of error correction codes for quantum computation. Quantum systems are inherently susceptible to errors due to environmental interactions or noise. Calculation-based analyses allow researchers to design and analyze error correction codes that mitigate these errors effectively. These studies involve intricate mathematical reasoning and simulation experiments to determine the optimal code parameters for fault-tolerant quantum computation.

In summary, calculation-based analyses in quantum computing enable researchers to delve into the theoretical foundations, algorithmic efficiency, error correction techniques, and computational complexities associated with this emerging field. Through sophisticated mathematical models and simulations, these analyses provide valuable insights into the capabilities and challenges of quantum computers while guiding further advancements in this rapidly evolving domain.

IX

Exploring the Subatomic World

The endeavour of delving into the depths of the subatomic realm necessitates an intricate and multidisciplinary approach. By employing cutting-edge technological apparatuses, such as particle accelerators and detectors, scientists embark upon a quest to unravel the fundamental constituents and interactions within matter. This captivating exploration entails studying particles that are smaller than an atom: encompassing quarks, leptons, and gauge bosons.

The Building Blocks of Matter

What is the Standard Model?

The Standard Model, a cornerstone of contemporary particle physics, constitutes an intricate theoretical framework that elucidates the subatomic realm. It embodies a comprehensive description of the fundamental particles and their interactions through three fundamental forces: the electromagnetic, weak, and strong forces. These interactions are mediated by force-carrying particles known as gauge bosons, which facilitate the exchange of energy and momentum between particles.

At its core, the Standard Model classifies elementary particles into two main categories: fermions and bosons. Fermions encompass quarks (constituents of protons and neutrons) and leptons (which include electrons and neutrinos). They obey the Pauli exclusion principle, rendering them subject to Fermi-Dirac statistics. In contrast, bosons govern the forces in nature and do not adhere to this principle. Notably, the Higgs boson plays a pivotal role within this framework by endowing other particles with mass.

While undeniably successful in explaining a vast array of experimental observations, the Standard Model leaves some questions unanswered. For instance, it does not account for gravity or offer an explanation for dark matter or dark energy, enigmatic phenomena that dominate our universe's composition. Hence, ongoing research endeavours strive to extend or supersede this model through frameworks such as supersymmetry or string theory in order to attain a more comprehensive understanding of the subatomic world's intricacies.

What are the different types of subatomic particles?

We encounter elementary particles, which are indivisible and devoid of internal structure. Examples include quarks, leptons, and gauge bosons. Quarks are the fundamental constituents of protons and neutrons, possessing fractional electric charges, while leptons comprise electrons and neutrinos. Gauge bosons mediate interactions between elementary particles, such as photons responsible for electromagnetic forces.

Quarks: These enigmatic entities represent the building blocks of matter, exhibiting an intrinsic form of near-zero size and colossal energy. Existing in six distinct flavours: up, down, charm, strange, top, and bottom, quarks possess fractional electric charges and interact via strong nuclear forces mediated by gluons. Their fascinating capacity for combining in groups of two or three forms composite particles known as hadrons, which encompass both mesons (quark-antiquark pairs) and baryons (three quarks). The interplay between quarks and their confinement within hadrons constitutes an enthralling field of study in modern particle physics.

Leptons: Residing outside the influence of strong nuclear forces, leptons are characterised by their minuscule masses and indivisibility into smaller components. This family features six members, the electron, muon, tauon, electron neutrino, muon neutrino, and tau neutrino, each carrying a unique charge and exhibiting weak interactions mediated by W and Z bosons.

What is the structure of an atom?

Contemporary atomic models built upon centuries of theoretical advancements propose a nucleus at the atom's centre, consisting of positively charged protons and uncharged neutrons. Surrounding this central core, negatively charged electrons occupy distinct energy levels or orbitals. These orbitals delineate regions where electron probability is highest, forming an electron cloud that envelops the nucleus.

What are the different theories describing the structure of matter?

Standard Model: Outlines a detailed classification of elementary particles and their interactions. According to this theory, matter is made up of fundamental particles called quarks and leptons, which combine to form larger particles like protons and neutrons. These particles interact with each other through four fundamental forces: electromagnetism, weak nuclear force, strong nuclear force, and gravity. However, while the Standard Model has been immensely successful in explaining a wide range of phenomena at the subatomic level, it still leaves certain questions unanswered.

Supersymmetry: This theory posits that every particle in the Standard Model has a counterpart or superpartner with different spin properties. Supersymmetry could provide a solution to some long-standing problems in physics and potentially unify all known forces into one grand unified theory. However, despite its promising potential implications for particle physics and cosmology, experimental evidence for supersymmetric particles has not yet been found.

Quantum field theory: It combines quantum mechanics with special relativity to describe how fields interact with particles and propagate through spacetime. According to this theory, all fundamental particles are excitations of various fields present throughout space. The concept of quantum fields allows for an elegant explanation of particle creation and annihilation processes as well as provides insight into phenomena such as antimatter.

What is the difference between fermions and bosons?

Bosons diverge from this paradigm by following an altogether different set of principles. In contrast to fermions, bosons readily embrace identical quantum states and willingly coexist in large numbers without resistance. This peculiar characteristic stems from their affiliation with integer spin values (0, 1, 2...), which grants them immunity against the constraints imposed by the Pauli exclusion principle. As a consequence of this more sociable nature, bosonic particles can engage in collective behaviour en masse, a trait often manifested through phenomena like superconductivity or superfluidity

X

Numerical Modelling of Physical Processes

The field of numerical modelling of physical processes encompasses the application of sophisticated mathematical techniques and computational algorithms to simulate and analyse a wide range of complex physical phenomena.

Numerical modelling

Quantum computing represents a significant departure from classical rules of computation. The key to understanding quantum computing lies in grasping the nature of quantum bits or qubits. Unlike classical bits, which can assume a value of either 0 or 1, qubits can exist in a superposition of states. When used in computations, this ability of qubits allows quantum computers to perform an enormous number of calculations simultaneously.

Numerical modelling of physical processes is the use of mathematical models to simulate phenomena. In quantum computing, this takes the form of quantifying the state of qubits. This representation draws heavily from quantum mechanics, which is a branch of physics that interprets physical phenomena at the most fundamental level. By truly marrying physics with computer science, the advent of quantum computing has given rise to essential concepts such as quantum state vectors and matrices, quantum entanglement, superposition, and quantum gates.

The application of quantum computing in the numerical modelling of physical processes has been cutting-edge. Quantum algorithms such as the Quantum Fourier Transform, which underpins the famous Shor's algorithm, have the potential to handle computations that would be untenable for classical computers. These calculations include the factoring of large prime numbers, used in data encryptions. Quantum computing can model physical systems with a greater degree of accuracy and effectiveness than classical computing.

In today's high-technology industries, many technological processes are described in terms of the Schrödinger equation. However, it is impossible to solve this equation exactly for a system with more than two particles, and this challenge introduces roadblocks for classical calculations. Quantum computers appear well prepared to handle this problem, showcasing a promising path towards modelling and simulation of multiple-particle systems.

The importance of quantum computers in numerical modelling becomes even more apparent when considering quantum simulations. Quantum simulations use quantum computers to simulate other quantum systems. This quality offers unprecedented retrieval of knowledge about the quantum world, paving the way for advancements in many fields such as materials science and pharmaceuticals. Currently, researchers are working on quantum algorithms to simulate molecule properties, advancing our understanding of complex chemical reactions.

While we are still in the early stages of quantum computing, the potential it holds for numerical modelling of physical processes is vast. It is postulated that quantum computing could be the key to unlock modelling of highly complex systems like climate modelling, intricate chemical processes, and more. However, reaching this potential comes with its own set of challenges such as achieving fault-tolerant quantum computing and making the technology more accessible to diverse sectors.

Finite Difference Methods

Quantum algorithms designed for specific problem domains exploit these unique properties to solve complex computations more efficiently than classical counterparts.

When it comes to numerically modelling physical processes, one commonly employed technique is Finite Difference Methods (FDMs). FDMs discretize continuous mathematical models into a set of finite difference equations that approximate derivatives in space and time. By dividing the domain into a grid, these methods allow us to efficiently calculate approximations for differential equations governing various physical phenomena. For instance, the heat equation describing thermal diffusion can be solved using FDMs by discretizing both time and space variables. The temperature at each grid point is then iteratively updated based on neighbouring points until a stable solution is reached.

To illustrate further, consider simulating wave propagation via FDMs. By discretizing both space and time dimensions into grids, we can approximate partial differential equations governing wave behaviour such as the wave equation or Helmholtz equation.

Monte Carlo Methods

Monte Carlo methods are a class of these techniques that rely on random sampling and statistical analysis to solve problems involving uncertainty or randomness in physical systems. These methods involve generating a series of random numbers and utilising them to simulate the behaviour of physical processes.

To illustrate this concept, consider the simulation of particle interactions in high-energy physics experiments. A numerical model employing Monte Carlo techniques can be employed to simulate the behaviour of particles within an accelerator or detector, taking into account various factors such as scattering, decay, and energy deposition. By leveraging quantum computing, one could potentially enhance these simulations by leveraging the inherent parallelism and exponential processing power offered by qubits. This combination may allow for more accurate predictions and faster analysis of experimental data in fields like particle physics or materials science.

Meshless Methods

In the context of numerical modelling using physical meshless methods, quantum computing offers tremendous potential. Meshless methods are computational techniques used to solve complex physical problems without explicit dependence on a predefined grid or mesh. By harnessing the power of quantum computation, numerical simulations based on physical meshless methods can achieve enhanced accuracy and efficiency for various applications such as fluid dynamics, electromagnetic field analysis, and molecular dynamics simulations.

For instance, consider a simulation of fluid flow around an aircraft wing using a meshless method called smoothed particle hydrodynamics (SPH). Quantum computing can significantly accelerate SPH calculations by leveraging its inherent parallelism and handling large amounts of data simultaneously. Such advancements enable researchers and engineers to obtain more accurate predictions of aerodynamic forces acting on the wing under different operating conditions. Similarly, in molecular dynamics simulations involving complex protein folding patterns or chemical reactions, quantum computing's capability for efficient parallel processing can dramatically reduce the computational time required for obtaining reliable results.

Discontinuous Galerkin Methods

Discontinuous Galerkin methods are numerical techniques used to discretize partial differential equations (PDEs) by splitting the computational domain into discontinuous elements. Quantum computers can efficiently handle large-scale systems involving multiple PDEs and unknowns, enabling accurate simulations and predictions of physical phenomena.

For instance, consider a scenario where we aim to model fluid dynamics using discontinuous Galerkin methods on a quantum computer. The complex interactions between different fluid elements can be represented as a set of PDEs with numerous unknown variables. By leveraging the parallel processing capabilities of quantum computing, we can efficiently solve these equations and obtain detailed insights into the behaviour of fluids under specific conditions, such as turbulent flows or multiphase systems. Such advancements in numerical modelling through quantum computing have the potential to revolutionise scientific research across multiple disciplines by providing more accurate predictions and enabling simulations that were previously computationally infeasible.

Lattice Boltzmann Methods

Numerical modelling in the context of physical lattice Boltzmann methods (LBM) refers to employing computational techniques to simulate fluid flows and other physical phenomena governed by the Boltzmann equation. LBM discretizes space into a lattice structure and assigns distribution functions to each lattice point, representing various particle populations. These distribution functions evolve over time according to collision and propagation rules, leading to macroscopic fluid behaviour.

By combining quantum computing with numerical modelling techniques such as LBM, researchers aim to harness the immense computational power offered by qubits for simulating complex physical systems. For instance, one could simulate fluid flow through a porous medium at an unprecedented scale or investigate complex fluid dynamics phenomena like turbulence.

Stochastic Methods

Stochastic methods are used when deterministic approaches are inadequate due to the presence of uncertainties or random fluctuations. These methods rely on statistical principles and probability theory to model and analyse different aspects of physical systems accurately.

To illustrate this concept, consider a Monte Carlo simulation used in financial markets. In this case, numerical modelling is employed to predict stock price movements by incorporating various stochastic factors, such as market volatility and random investor behaviour. By repeatedly sampling from a probability distribution function, the simulation provides insights into potential outcomes with varying probabilities. Another example is molecular dynamics simulations used in chemistry or materials science research, where numerical models incorporate stochastic elements to account for thermal fluctuations in atomic motions.

Parallel Computing

Numerical modelling involves constructing mathematical representations of physical systems to simulate their behaviour. In the context of quantum computing, numerical modelling plays a crucial role in understanding and optimising the performance of various parallel computing methods used in this domain. These methods include algorithms like Shor's algorithm for prime factorization and Grover's algorithm for searching an unsorted database. By employing numerical models, researchers can analyse the efficiency and scalability of these algorithms on different quantum systems, enabling them to anticipate challenges and devise solutions.

For example, suppose we consider Shor's algorithm used for breaking RSA encryption. Numerical modelling would involve constructing a mathematical framework that simulates the behaviour of qubits during each step of the factoring process. This model would allow us to investigate factors like noise, decoherence, and gate error rates affecting the algorithm's performance. By manipulating various parameters within this model, we can assess how different factors impact efficiency and identify strategies to mitigate their influence. Ultimately, numerical modelling provides valuable insights into harnessing the power of physical parallel computing methods offered by quantum computing technology.

XI

Quantum Simulation of Complex Systems

The concept of quantum simulation of complex systems refers to the utilisation of quantum mechanical systems to emulate and investigate intricate phenomena that are difficult to comprehend or analyse using classical methods.

Types of Quantum Simulations

Quantum simulations encompass a broad array of computational techniques employed to elucidate and comprehend complex physical phenomena in quantum systems. These simulations can be categorised into various types based on their underlying principles and methodologies. One such classification is based on the level of abstraction utilised in these simulations. In high-level quantum simulations, an abstract representation of the system is employed, which enables researchers to investigate general properties and behaviour without delving into intricate details. This approach often leverages mathematical models and algorithms to provide valuable insights into the macroscopic behaviour of quantum systems.

Another category within quantum simulations is low-level or microscopic simulations, where a more detailed representation of the system is employed. Such simulations aim to capture the most granular aspects of the quantum system, accounting for particle interactions, energy exchanges, and other microscopic phenomena. This level of simulation requires significant computational resources due to its high dimensionality and complexity but allows researchers to obtain a more accurate understanding of specific processes occurring at the microscale.

Additionally, one may consider hybrid quantum simulations that combine elements from both high-level and low-level approaches. Hybrid simulations leverage simplified models for certain parts of a system while incorporating more detailed descriptions for others. By striking a balance between computational efficiency and accuracy, hybrid approaches offer a pragmatic compromise for investigating complex quantum phenomena.

Applications of Quantum Simulations

The current discourse on the subject of quantum simulations harbours a plethora of intriguing applications that have captivated the attention of researchers across various scientific disciplines. Quantum simulations entail emulation and analysis of quantum systems, which exhibit complex behaviour beyond the scope of classical computing techniques. One prominent application lies in the realm of condensed matter physics, where scientists endeavour to elucidate the properties and dynamics of materials at atomic and subatomic scales. By leveraging quantum simulators, researchers can effectively model intricate phenomena such as superconductivity, magnetism, and topological phases, thereby unravelling fundamental mechanisms underlying material behaviour.

Another significant area where quantum simulations demonstrate immense potential is in computational chemistry. Conventional methods often fail to accurately predict molecular structures, reaction rates, and electronic properties due to their limitations in accounting for strong correlation effects and quantum tunnelling phenomena. Quantum simulators offer an alternative avenue by enabling precise calculations of chemical systems with remarkable accuracy. Through exploring chemical reactions and interactions at a quantum level, these simulations facilitate the development of novel catalysts, drugs, and materials with enhanced efficiency and functionality.

Moreover, the field of optimization has also witnessed promising advancements through the incorporation of quantum simulations. Complex optimization problems encompass numerous fundamental challenges in diverse domains such as logistics planning, financial portfolio management, or machine learning algorithm design. By harnessing principles from quantum mechanics to develop quantum algorithms specifically tailored for optimization tasks, researchers have achieved substantial speedups compared to classical counterparts.

Applications of Quantum Simulations

The current discourse on the subject of quantum simulations harbours a plethora of intriguing applications that have captivated the attention of researchers across various scientific disciplines. Quantum simulations entail emulation and analysis of quantum systems, which exhibit complex behaviour beyond the scope of classical computing techniques. One prominent application lies in the realm of condensed matter physics, where scientists endeavour to elucidate the properties and dynamics of materials at atomic and subatomic scales. By leveraging quantum simulators, researchers can effectively model intricate phenomena such as superconductivity, magnetism, and topological phases, thereby unravelling fundamental mechanisms underlying material behaviour.

Another significant area where quantum simulations demonstrate immense potential is in computational chemistry. Conventional methods often fail to accurately predict molecular structures, reaction rates, and electronic properties due to their limitations in accounting for strong correlation effects and quantum tunnelling phenomena. Quantum simulators offer an alternative avenue by enabling precise calculations of chemical systems with remarkable accuracy. Through exploring chemical reactions and interactions at a quantum level, these simulations facilitate the development of novel catalysts, drugs, and materials with enhanced efficiency and functionality.

Moreover, the field of optimization has also witnessed promising advancements through the incorporation of quantum simulations. Complex optimization problems encompass numerous fundamental challenges in diverse domains such as logistics planning, financial portfolio management, or machine learning algorithm design. By harnessing principles from quantum mechanics to develop quantum algorithms specifically tailored for optimization tasks, researchers have achieved substantial speedups compared to classical counterparts.

Quantum Algorithms for Simulating Complex Systems

Quantum Algorithms for Simulation: An Overview

Quantum algorithms are computations designed for quantum computers. These algorithms predominantly use the challenges of complex quantum processes to solve complex computational problems. Quantum algorithms for simulating complex systems are relevant in fields such as chemistry, physics, biology, and materials science, wherein simulation helps understand the behaviour and evolution of complex systems.

Quantum Simulation: Impact and

Relevance

Quantum simulation assists in exploring the nature of matter on the fundamental level, including molecules and chemical reactions pivotal to drug discovery and materials science. These complex processes, challenging to model using classical systems, are innate to quantum computers due to their quantum nature.

Simulations such as these require the calculation of states and respective changes. Classical algorithms tend to require resources that increase exponentially with the system size. However, quantum algorithms can calculate these states more efficiently, making them increasingly relevant in simulating complex systems.

Quantum Algorithms: Examples and Applications

Several quantum algorithms actively contribute to simulating complex systems. The Quantum Phase Estimation algorithm is one, crucial for the simulation of quantum chemistry and physics phenomena. The Quantum Amplitude Estimation algorithm allows for accurate calculation of expected values, used in finance and machine learning. The Quantum Counting algorithm, meanwhile, allows for the determination of the cardinality of an input subset, relevant in database systems.

The simulation of quantum chemistry has been widely pursued, predicting the properties and behaviour of molecules. Quantum-based simulation can outperform classical means by calculating ground state energies and molecular properties more efficiently, positively impacting fields like drug discovery and materials design.

XII

Particle Tracking Simulations

Particle tracking simulations refer to computational models that are utilised to simulate the behaviour and movement of individual particles within a given system. These simulations serve as valuable tools in various scientific disciplines, particularly in fields such as fluid dynamics, environmental sciences, and biophysics.

Simulation of Particle Motion in Complex Flows

Understanding the motion of particles in complex flows has significant scientific and technological implications, ranging from developing clean energy technology to understanding environmental processes. Numerical particle tracking techniques reinforce the picture of particle motion in a complex flow. This article explores the simulation of particle motion in complex flows and presents a rudimentary code to provide a clear understanding of the subject.

Particles suspended in a fluid follow the fluid flow, until external forces or the particle's properties such as inertia and buoyancy come into play. The distinguishing features of particle behaviour in complex flows often arise from a non-uniform or unsteady flow field.

Particle tracking algorithms are often employed to predict the trajectory of particles within complex flows. The force balance on the particle serves as the governing equation for motion, with drag, buoyancy, and external forces such as gravity being major considerations. In some cases, forces such as the Saffman's lift and virtual mass effect can become relevant.

Simulating particle motion in complex flows usually involves integrating the governing equation over time. This can be challenging since the forces associated with particle motion can be nonlinear, leading to unstable numerical solutions.

Carefully selecting an appropriate time integration scheme is, therefore, crucial. The two commonly used methods include the Euler method and the Verlet method.

Let's consider a simple code for particle simulation in Python:

```python
# Simple Particle Tracking Code

import numpy as np

# Initialize particle position and velocity

r = np.array([0.0, 0.0, 0.0]) # position

v = np.array([1.0, 0.0, 0.0]) # velocity

# Initialize time and time step

t = 0.0

dt = 0.01

# Numerical integration (Euler method)

for i in range(1000):

F = -0.01 * v # Drag force (proportional to velocity)

v = v + F * dt # Update velocity

r = r + v * dt # Update position

t = t + dt # Advance time
```

```
print('The final particle position is', r)

```

The code simulates the motion of a particle subject to a drag force proportional to its velocity in a single spatial dimension. The drag force -0.01*v models the resistance of the particle to the motion caused by its interaction with the surrounding fluid. The time integration uses the Euler method, where the new velocity is approximated via Newton's second law, and the new position is computed using the updated velocity.

Though the above code is a simple 1-dimensional example, in real applications, one would want to simulate the motion of a particle in a 3-dimensional flow field based on complex fluid dynamics.

Despite the evolving advancements in computing power, accurately simulating the motion of entrained particles in complex flow remains a challenge. Modern tools have aided in refining these simulation methodologies. Software like LIGGGHTS, EDEM, and Rocky dem are explicitly designed to simulate particle motion through a complex flow field.

The most pronounced development in this area, however, might be the advancements in GPU computing. By utilising large numbers of cores in a graphics processing unit (GPU), simulation times can be dramatically reduced. The innovation has seen the development of particle simulation software that runs entirely on the GPU, such as GPUSPH and DualSPHysics.

Having a solid understanding of how particles behave in complex flow mechanisms will continue to be invaluable across multiple industries, from medicine to renewable energy and environmental sciences. Further research would certainly offer continued progress into the simulation and control of particle motion in complex flows.

Modelling of Diffusion and Transport of Particles

The modelling of diffusion and transport of particles is a sophisticated discipline within the realm of applied mathematics and physics that examines the intricate mechanisms involved in the movement and dispersion of microscopic entities. This field employs complex mathematical frameworks and analytical techniques to describe the intricate processes associated with the motion and distribution of particles in various mediums.

One crucial aspect of particle transport is diffusion, a process that describes how particles spread from regions of high concentration to areas of lower concentration. Diffusion is a result of the random movement of particles and it can be described mathematically using Fick's laws of diffusion.

Fick's First Law of Diffusion

Fick's first law relates the diffusive flux to the concentration under the assumption of steady state. It postulates that the flux goes from regions of high concentration to regions of lower concentration, with a magnitude proportional to the concentration gradient. Its general form is expressed in the equation:

flux = -D * (dc/dx)

Where:

- Flux is the amount of substance transferred per unit area per unit time.

- D is the diffusion coefficient of diffusivity.

- dc/dx is the concentration gradient.

Fick's Second Law of Diffusion

Fick's second law predicts how diffusion causes the concentration to change with time. It is a second-order differential equation, mathematically complex, that describes the rate of change in concentration as a function of position and time:

$$\partial c/\partial t = D * (d^2c/dx^2)$$

Where:

- $\partial c/\partial t$ is the rate of change of concentration with time

- D is the diffusion coefficient of diffusivity

- d^2c/dx^2 is the second derivative of the concentration with respect to position, a measure of its curvature.

In many practical applications, the transport of particles is not limited to diffusion. For instance, in fluvial systems or aerosols, advection or the transport due to the bulk motion of the fluid can be just as significant, if not more so.

Advection-Diffusion Equation

The phenomenon of advection, in combination with diffusion, results in a more complex process. The continuous, deterministic advection-diffusion equation describes how tinges of particles will move in a fluid and it can be written as:

$$\partial c/\partial t + v * (\partial c/\partial x) = D * (d^2 c/dx^2)$$

Where:

- $\partial c/\partial t$ is the change in concentration with time

- v is the velocity of the fluid

- $\partial c/\partial x$ is the gradient of concentration

- D is the diffusion coefficient

- $d^2 c/dx^2$ is the second spatial derivative of concentration.

These mathematical models form the foundation for understanding and predicting the diffusion and transport of particles. However, the complexity lies in solving these equations. Analytical solutions, while they offer precise prospective, are unfeasible for anything but the simplest scenarios. Therefore, numerical solutions often become the most practicable approach to solve these equations. These solutions can be executed using various numerical methods, including Finite Difference Method (FDM), Finite Element Method (FEM), and Finite Volume Method (FVM).

Numerical simulation of particle transport modelling using software, such as MATLAB or Python with libraries like SciPy and Numpy, offers a powerful tool for researchers. They can create precise models that simulate the diffusion and transport of particles in various contexts, allowing them to better understand and make predictions about these complex systems.

Analysis of Turbulence and Particles

Turbulence, a complex physical phenomenon, appears in various natural and artificial systems such as atmospheric weather patterns, turbulent flow in pipes, plasma fusion, and many more. In fluid dynamics, turbulence refers to a disordered state of flow laden with eddies, swirls, and chaotic changes in velocity and pressure. This particular state hinders the accurate prediction of fluid flow characteristics, complicating the study and design of fluid systems.

Particle behaviour in turbulence, an equally significant topic, has attracted substantial attention for many decades. Studying particles in turbulence is valuable in a wide range of scientific fields, including climatology due to the critical role that aerosol particles play in cloud formation and precipitation.

The various approaches used for the analysis of turbulence include the Direct Numerical Simulation (DNS), Large Eddy Simulation (LES), and Reynolds Averaged Navier-Stokes equation (RANS). Using these advanced computational methods, engineers and scientists can analyse and predict complex turbulent flows.

Understanding the interaction between turbulence and particles is crucial in many technical applications such as multiphase flows and pollutant dispersion. For instance, multiphase flow, where the flow has more than one phase (gas, liquid, solid), like sediment transportation in rivers and combustion processes in engines.

Aerosol scientists have shown that the size of the particles affects their behaviour in turbulence quite significantly. With smaller particles tending to follow the fluid's motion closely, known as behaving 'passively,' whereas larger particles are more affected by turbulence. Moreover, the size, density, and shape of particles can all influence their dispersion, settling velocity, and distribution in turbulence.

Numerical Simulation of Particle-Laden Flows

Numerical simulation is an instrumental tool in understanding and predicting the behaviour of fluid dynamics and particle-laden flows. It encompasses a myriad of real-world applications such as sediment transport, aerosol dispersion and industrial particulate processes, elucidating the importance of continuous research and innovation in this field.

Particle-laden flows ideally occur when particles are suspended in a fluid, forming a composition where the dynamics of each phase influences the other. Mathematical models and numerical techniques, hence, are crucial in accurately simulating these intricate systems.

One of the commonly used numerical models to simulate particle-laden flows is the Euler-Lagrange method. This approach handles the fluid phase as a continuum described by the Eulerian formulation of the Navier-Stokes equations, while treating the discrete phase, the particles, in a Lagrangian framework; where each particle's motion is individually solved.

Following is an illustrative Python code implementing a simple 2D Euler-Lagrange particle-laden flow simulation:

```Python
# Euler-Lagrange 2D Particle-Laden Flow Simulation
```

```
import numpy as np

def euler_lagrange_simulation(particles, fluid, timestep,
run_time):

for t in np.arange(0, run_time, timestep):

fluid.update_fluid_field(timestep)

for particle in particles:

particle.update_particle_position(timestep, fluid)

```
```

In this abecedarian illustration, fluid and particles are objects representing the fluid phase and the discrete phase (particles) respectively. The fluid's field is updated according to the Eulerian framework, while each particle's position is updated using the Lagrangian approach.

Another key numerical model employed for simulations is the Euler-Euler model. This model regards both the fluid and the particle phase as interpenetrating continua, described by sets of averaged conservation equations which serve to eliminate computational intensiveness brought about by tracking individual particles.

Notwithstanding the applicability of these numerical models, aspects like fluid-particle interaction, turbulence and transport of discrete phase are still challenging to accommodate within these frameworks. For instance,
```

interactions between particles and turbulence can significantly influence the dynamics of particle-laden flows.

Therefore, Direct Numerical Simulation (DNS) combined with a Lagrangian point-particle tracking methodology is increasingly gaining traction. DNS resolves all scales of fluid motion, allowing detailed analysis and improved understanding of the underlying physics of particle-laden flows.

Nevertheless, the particle-based nature of DNS makes it computationally expensive, particularly for high Reynolds number flows and dense particulate systems. Subsequently, coarser levels of description, such as Large-Eddy Simulation (LES) and Reynolds-Averaged Navier-Stokes (RANS) methods, are often employed, albeit at the expense of some detailed physics.

The onset of this research frontier leaves space for improvements and refinements. Future advancements hinge on the development of numerical techniques that minimise approximation while maximising computational efficiency, making the precise simulation of particle-laden flows a more practical and effective proposition.

Particle-Laden Flow Dynamics

Particle-Laden Flow Dynamics (PLFD) analyses the behaviour and motion of solid particles within fluid flows. Crucial across a variety of industries, it attends to phenomena such as particle transport, sedimentation, and erosion. An accurate understanding of PLFD can aid in improving pipeline efficiencies, pollution control, and various multiphase flow applications.

The interaction of particles and fluids is complex, with numerous factors impacting resultant behaviour. Among these are the particle size and distribution, fluid viscosity and density, and the external forces acting upon the system. The comprehensive study of PLFD thus requires simultaneous consideration of all these parameters, with multiple experimental techniques and numerical simulations in use.

Navier-Stokes equations are generally used to model the behaviour of continuous fluid flows, yet they fall short when applied to PLFD. Thus, the study of PLFD yields to more specialised models encompassing the Euler-Lagrange and Euler-Euler methods.

The Euler-Lagrange method, also known as the discrete particle method, assumes that the number of particles is relatively small compared to the volume of fluid. It solves the Navier-Stokes equations for the fluid phase and Newton's second law for the dispersed phase.

This method can be expressed in mathematical form:

Momentum equation:

$$F_p = m \, d(v_d/dt)$$

Where F_p is the force experienced by the particle, m is the mass of the particle, v_d is the velocity of the particle, and dt is time.

The Euler-Euler method, or the two-fluid model, considers both phases as interpenetrating continua. This method solves the momentum and continuity equations for each phase, accounting for interphase exchange terms vital to achieve accurate results.

The simplified continuity and momentum equations for both fluids and particles can be written as:

Continuity equation:

$$\partial(\varepsilon_p \rho_p)/\partial t + \nabla \cdot (\varepsilon_p \rho_p u) = 0$$

Momentum equation:

$$\partial(\varepsilon_p \rho_p u)/\partial t + \nabla \cdot (\varepsilon_p \rho_p u u) = -\varepsilon_p \nabla P + \varepsilon_p \rho_p g - \nabla \cdot (\varepsilon_p \tau_p)$$

Where ε_p is the volume fraction, ρ_p is the density, u is the velocity, P is the pressure, g is the acceleration due to gravity, and τ_p is the Cauchy stress tensor.

Despite its complexity, the study of PLFD opens the door to innovations across industries, enhancing efficiency and developing sustainable solutions. Continuous advancements in this field thus remain vital to engineering progress.

Validation and Verification of Particle Tracking Simulations

Particle tracking simulations play a significant role in computational science and engineering. These simulations make it possible to gain insights into physical phenomena that would otherwise be expensive, impossible, or unsafe to investigate in the real world. Verification and Validation (V&V) processes are essential for ensuring the accuracy and reliability of the results produced by these simulations. Verification ensures the code correctly implements the simulation, while validation ensures that the simulation correctly predicts physical behaviour.

Verification of Particle Tracking Simulations

Code verification involves rigorous comparison of the implemented algorithm and the mathematical model that it represents. An example of verification is the method of manufactured solutions (MMS), a popular option that involves creating an artificial exact solution and adjusting the source terms to conform to that solution while satisfying the governing equations.

First, a theoretical solution is manufactured, after which the algorithm model equations are applied so they match the manufactured solution. For example, in Python code, you might create a hypothetical solution with the Numpy library:

```python
import numpy as np

x = np.linspace(-1, 1, 1000)

y = np.linspace(-1, 1, 1000)

xx, yy = np.meshgrid(x, y)

u_exact = np.sin(np.pi*xx) * np.sin(np.pi*yy)
```

Then, you might adjust the right-hand side of the equations to match the manufactured solution:

```python
f = -2 * np.pi**2 * np.sin(np.pi*xx) * np.sin(np.pi*yy)
```

The error between the numerical and exact solutions checks the accuracy of the implemented algorithm:

```python
u_numeric = solve_poisson_equation(f) # Poisson solver not defined here

error = np.linalg.norm(u_numeric - u_exact, np.inf)
```

If the error obtained is within an acceptable tolerance, the code verification is successful.

Validation of Particle Tracking Simulations

Validation, on the other hand, involves comparing simulation results with experimental or empirical data to determine if the simulation is capable of predicting real-world performance. This process can be considerably more complicated, as it requires extensive and accurate data for comparison.

Nevertheless, a common code validation approach involves constructing a data comparison framework where the simulation and empirical data are directly compared. In Python again for instance, you might import experimental data using the Pandas library:

```python
import pandas as pd

exp_data = pd.read_csv('exp_data.csv')
```

Then, you compare the simulation results with the experimental data:

```python
```

```
sim_data = run_simulation() # Simulation runner not
defined here

diff = np.abs(sim_data - exp_data)

max_diff = np.max(diff)

```

If the maximum difference (or some other metric) is within the acceptable tolerance, the validation is successful.

Parameter Estimation for Particle Tracking Simulations

Parameter estimation works on the premise of stochastic processes, wherein a random or probabilistic scenario is considered to describe the behaviour of particles. These parameters might include factors such as velocity, displacement, concentration, etc. In particle tracking, this facet is crucial to mirror the intricacies of actual systems accurately.

Parameter estimation in particle tracking simulation can be achieved through various techniques. One of the most widely utilised methods is the Maximum Likelihood Estimation (MLE). Fundamentally, MLE determines the parameters that maximise the likelihood function, making the observed data most probable.

For instance, if we represent the particle's displacement as random variables following a normal distribution, the MLE computation can be carried out using Python:

```python
import numpy as np

from scipy.stats import norm

# Simulated displacement data

data = np.random.normal(0, 1, 1000)
```

```python
# MLE for mean and standard deviation

mu, std = norm.fit(data)

print(f'Mean = {mu}, Std Dev = {std}')

```
```

The output will return the estimated parameters, mean (mu) and standard deviation (std), for the normal distribution of the data.

Another common method involves the usage of Bayesian Inference, which updates the probability of a hypothesis as more evidence becomes available. This method can elegantly be implemented as:

```python
import pymc3 as pm

data = [...]

with pm.Model() as model:

# Prior distribution

mu = pm.Normal('mu', mu=0, sd=1)

sigma = pm.HalfNormal('sigma', sd=1)

# Likelihood

likelihood = pm.Normal('likelihood', mu=mu, sd=sigma, observed=data)
```
```

```
# MCMC sampling

trace = pm.sample(2000, tune=1000)

```
```

Theoretically, these parameter estimation methods provide a probabilistic understanding of the system's behaviour under consideration. From a practical perspective, they aid in ascertaining the accuracy of simulations and this subsequently facilitates significant advancements in respective domains.

However, there is a persisting need to make these estimations more robust and reliable to ensure that these simulations can predict real-world phenomena with increased reliability and precision. This calls for the evolution of more advanced algorithms dedicated to parameter estimation in particle tracking simulations.
```

XIII

Algorithmic Optimizations for Solving Physics Problems

The present discourse delves into a comprehensive investigation of algorithmic optimizations applied to the resolution of physics problems. The overarching objective is to enhance computational efficacy and improve accuracy in the modelling and simulation of physical phenomena.

Particle Swarm Optimization

Solving complex physics problems has always been a demanding task. It involves careful examination and identification of correct parameters, deploying appropriate methods and meticulously analysing the results for achieving accurate conclusions. With the intervention of modern technologies such as Artificial Intelligence (AI) and Machine Learning (ML), the process of resolving these complex physics problems has taken a paradigm shift. One such technique is the Particle Swarm Optimization (PSO) algorithm, a quintessential AI-driven tool that has been proven beneficial in solving physics problems.

Developed by James Kennedy and Russell Eberhart in 1995, the PSO algorithm exemplifies population-based stochastic optimization techniques. It simulates the social behaviour of organisms, such as bird flocking or fish schooling. The primary goal in PSO is to optimise a given function where each 'particle' in the swarm represents a potential solution. These particles fly through the hyperspace and are attracted by the best locations they have reached, gradually converging to the optimal solution.

The PSO algorithm has its roots in physics, notably in the computational modelling of problems such as minimization of energy and optimization of wave functions. These challenges require obtaining the global minimum of a high-dimensional and complex energy landscape. PSO assists in such cases by providing a simple yet powerful heuristic, positioning it as a natural choice for these problems.

There are numerous examples in physics where PSO has facilitated in finding solutions. Case in point, nuclear spectroscopy, which involves interactive adjustment of parameters to gain optimal values that can correspond to experimental data, sees a significant benefit from this algorithm. In addition, PSO has been significantly utilised in electromagnetism for tuning antenna element weights, optimising reflectarray antenna design, and suppressing side lobe levels.

Despite the benefits, one should not overlook the shortfalls of PSO. It is sensitive to initial settings and parameter selection, and it tends to get stuck in local minima in some high-dimensional problems. Notwithstanding these shortcomings, PSO's benefits in ease of implementation, fewer parameters to adjust, and simplicity make it a strong contender in solving an array of physics problems.

Simulated Annealing

Simulated annealing employs a probabilistic acceptance criterion, allowing it to effectively escape local optima and explore global solution spaces. By utilising the Metropolis criterion, which considers both uphill moves and downhill moves, simulated annealing can intelligently navigate through rugged energy landscapes in physics problems. Additionally, temperature plays a crucial role as an exploration parameter in simulated annealing, as it controls the probability of accepting solutions with higher energies.

To further enhance the efficiency of simulated annealing, various algorithmic optimizations have been proposed. These optimizations include adaptive cooling schedules, parallelization techniques, and neighbourhood strategies for exploring nearby solutions efficiently. Adaptive cooling schedules dynamically adjust the temperature during the optimization process based on problem-specific characteristics or statistical analysis of previous iterations. Parallelization techniques exploit multiple computing resources to perform simultaneous exploration of different regions within the search space, improving both speed and accuracy. Lastly, clever neighbourhood strategies help guide the search towards promising regions by intelligently selecting neighbouring states for evaluation.

Reinforcement Learning

The current discourse revolves around the application of algorithmic optimizations in the realm of physics problem-solving, with a particular focus on the integration of reinforcement learning methodologies. This cutting-edge approach aims to enhance computational efficiency and accuracy in tackling complex physics conundrums. By leveraging a combination of sophisticated algorithms and reinforcement learning techniques, researchers aim to expedite the process of identifying optimal solutions for intricate physics problems.

One key aspect of this research involves the utilisation of algorithmic optimizations, which are advanced techniques that streamline computational processes by reducing inefficiencies. These optimizations entail refining existing algorithms or devising novel ones specifically tailored to address the intricacies inherent in physics problem-solving. The ultimate objective is to facilitate rapid and accurate identification of solutions while minimising computational resources.

In parallel, reinforcement learning techniques are employed as a complementary approach within this domain. Reinforcement learning involves an iterative process where an agent learns from its interactions with the environment to make sequential decisions and optimise its performance over time. By incorporating such methods into the framework, researchers endeavour to improve adaptive decision-making capabilities and optimise outcomes when solving complex physics problems. This integration allows for more efficient exploration of solution spaces, paving the way for advancements in diverse fields such as astrophysics, quantum mechanics, and particle physics.

XIV

Data Mining and Predictive Analytics

Data mining is a sophisticated computational technique that encompasses a diverse array of statistical and machine learning methods to extract meaningful patterns and knowledge from large datasets. It involves the systematic exploration and analysis of vast amounts of data to identify hidden relationships, correlations, and trends that may have previously eluded human perception.

Statistical Modelling

In the ever-evolving world of data-driven decision-making, two concepts that stand out are Data Mining and Predictive Analytics. These branches of statistics leverage mathematical computations and present insights that assist businesses to make informed decisions.

Data Mining refers to the process of discovering patterns within vast chunks of data involving methods at the intersection of machine learning, statistics, and database management. These patterns typically serve as a valuable resource that allows analysts and decision-makers to draw verifiable hypotheses and unearth valuable insights. On the other hand, Predictive Analytics uses historical and current data to make predictions about future or otherwise unknown events. It often employs statistical algorithms and machine learning techniques to determine the likelihood of future outcomes.

Statistical modelling plays a critical role in both Data Mining and Predictive Analytics. For instance, in Data Mining, analysts often utilise mathematical algorithms to extract patterns from broad datasets. Regressions, decision trees, and clustering are among the common methods applied.

Regression analysis is a set of statistical methods used for the estimation of relationships among variables. It includes many techniques for modelling and analysing several variables, when the focus is on the relationship between a dependent variable and one or more independent variables.

Decision Trees, on the other hand, are simple, yet effective, they compartmentalise data into distinct categories based on certain predetermined variables. These models are powerful tools for classification and prediction problems because they mimic human decision-making more closely compared to other algorithms.

Clustering involves the task of dividing the data points into several groups such that data points in the same groups are more similar to other data points in the same group and dissimilar to the data points in other groups. It is basically a collection of objects based on similarity and dissimilarity between them.

In Predictive Analytics, mathematical models are applied to anticipate future trends or behaviours. For instance, the Linear Regression model is used to identify the relationship between two or more variables. Thereafter, analysts use the model to predict a dependent variable based on a given independent variable.

Also, Logistic Regression and Naïve Bayes are some of the widely used predictive models. The Logistic Regression model is typically used for binary classification problems. Whereas, Naïve Bayes classifiers are a family of simple "probabilistic classifiers" based on applying Bayes' theorem with strong independence assumptions between the features.

Time Series Analysis

Time Series Analysis structures data into a pattern that elucidates the hidden underlying mechanisms driving the observations.

The main purpose of Time Series Analysis is to map trends and patterns that occur sequentially over time and subsequently formulate reliable models to predict future values accurately. The intrinsic value of working with sequenced data is the ability to identify persistent patterns, occasional irregularities, and long-term trends that are not readily discernible in isolated, random data points.

Time Series Analysis is structured around four main components: the trend-cycle, seasonal, irregular, and cyclical components. The trend-cycle component portrays the long-term progression of the series and allows for both trend (direction and rate of alteration) and cycle (oscillations happening as a result of economic conditions). The seasonal component indicates repetitive short-term cycling within a year, the irregular component covers the erratic or random fluctuations, and the cyclical component represents oscillations driven by business cycles lasting more than a year.

Applying statistical tools for Time Series Analysis primarily involves methods like Autoregressive Integrated Moving Average (ARIMA) and Exponential Smoothing. ARIMA models are capable of fitting different types of time series data. ARIMA is characterised by three parameters: 'order of the autoregressive model (p)', 'order of differencing (d)', and 'order of moving average model (q)'. The model adopts a step-by-step approach starting with making the series stationary and then identifying the appropriate values for p, d, and q.

On the other hand, Exponential Smoothing is used to forecast data points by calculating the weighted averages of past observations, with weights declining exponentially. The most recent observations have higher weights compared to older ones: the rate of decrease is a function of a constant called the 'smoothing constant', denoted by α, ranging between 0 and 1.

Decision Tree Learning

Decision tree learning is a prominent methodology in machine learning, encompassing a diverse range of algorithms that aim to construct decision trees from labelled training data. This approach involves partitioning the feature space into regions based on specific attribute values and making informed decisions at each partition based on the associated class labels. The construction process involves recursively splitting the data, employing various metrics such as entropy or Gini impurity, which quantifies the uncertainty or disorder within a given set of instances.

The underlying principles of decision tree learning borrow from information theory and statistical inference techniques. By effectively evaluating and comparing attribute values, decision trees can efficiently capture complex non-linear relationships between input features and target variables. This allows for interpretability as the resulting decision tree can be visualised with clear paths representing distinct decision-making rules. However, the drawback lies in their susceptibility to overfitting, where excessively complex trees may adapt too closely to the training data but struggle with generalisation when exposed to unseen instances.

To mitigate this issue, various strategies exist such as pruning, which reduces unnecessary branches or nodes that do not contribute significantly to classification accuracy. Additionally, ensemble methods like random forests leverage multiple decision trees to enhance predictive performance by aggregating their outputs. Despite their inherent limitations, decision tree learning remains a valuable tool in many domains due to its interpretability and ability to handle both categorical and continuous attributes effectively.

Neural Networks and Deep Learning

In the era of rapid technological advancements, the terms 'Artificial Intelligence' (AI), 'Machine Learning' (ML), 'Neural Networks' (NN), and 'Deep Learning' (DL) have become cardinal entities. Among these, neural networks and deep learning have positioned themselves as the underpinning technologies driving the AI revolution.

Understanding Neural Networks

Neural networks, also known as artificial neural networks (ANNs), imitate the structure and function of the human brain to process data. An ANN comprises interconnected layers of nodes or "neurons" which receive, process, and transmit information using deliberate weight adjustments - making the network "learn".

```python
#importing libraries

import tensorflow as tf

from tensorflow.keras.models import Sequential

from tensorflow.keras.layers import Dense

# setting up a neural network

model = Sequential()
```

```python
model.add(Dense(5, input_dim=8, activation='relu'))  # Input layer

model.add(Dense(10, activation='relu')) # Hidden layer

model.add(Dense(1, activation='sigmoid')) # Output layer
```

With a basic sequential model in TensorFlow, the three layers of a neural network – the input, hidden, and the output layer are created using the Dense function. The activation function is specified with the 'relu' for non-linear transformation and 'sigmoid' for the output layer.

The Advent of Deep Learning

Deep Learning is a sub-field of ML and utilises artificial neural networks with multiple hidden layers. Each layer learns to transform its input data into more abstract and composite representations, hence 'going deeper'.

```python

#importing libraries

from tensorflow.keras.layers import Conv2D, Flatten

# setting up a deep learning model

model = Sequential()

model.add(Conv2D(32, (3,3), activation='relu', input_shape=(64, 64, 3))) # Convolution layer
```

```
model.add(Flatten()) # Flattening layer

model.add(Dense(128, activation='relu'))  # Fully connected layer

model.add(Dense(1, activation='sigmoid')) # Output layer
```
```

Here, a convolutional neural network (CNN), a type of deep learning model, is used for processing images. The Conv2D layer learns spatial hierarchies by applying a series of learnable filters. The output is flattened then passed through Dense layers.

## Applications and Future Perspective

From autonomous vehicles, speech recognition systems to enhancing medical diagnostics, neural networks and deep learning are transforming various industries. With continuous advancements, we can anticipate more intuitive, efficient algorithms leading to unprecedented applications.
```

XV

Uncovering the Mysteries of Quantum Mechanics

The elusive nature of particles in quantum systems demands novel approaches to comprehend their probabilistic behaviour and non-local correlations. Drawing upon mathematical formalisms like Dirac notation and linear algebraic manipulations, researchers engage in rigorous analysis to unravel these mysteries.

Introduction to Quantum Mechanics

Quantum Mechanics, often referred to as the quantum theory or quantum physics, is a fundamental theory in physics that provides a description of the physical properties of nature at the scale of atoms and subatomic particles. The term 'quantum mechanics' itself stems from the nature of energy in microscopic scales, which can only exist in indivisible units known as quanta ('quantum' in singular form).

Quantum mechanics has managed to revolutionise our understanding of the microscopic world. It emerged in the early 20th century from the failure of classical physics in explaining certain physical phenomena and experimental predictions related to the subatomic realm. These involve phenomena like the behaviour of black bodies, the photoelectric effect, and anomalies in the spectra emanating from heated gases.

In quantum mechanics, reality is different from what we are accustomed to in our daily experiences. The principles of quantum mechanics tell us that particles can exist in multiple places at once and even move forward and backward in time. Additionally, it is impossible to know the exact position and momentum of a particle at the same time, known as Heisenberg's uncertainty principle.

This new branch of physics brought a radical departure from Newtonian physics. Instead of declaring definite trajectories and outcomes, quantum mechanics introduced the concept of superposition. This means that a system can exist in several states at once – until a measurement or interaction forces it into one definite state.

So, how exactly do particles exist in several places at once? This concept is delicately explained by Schrödinger's wave equations. According to Schrödinger, particles don't have specific positions, rather they exist in a cloud of probabilities. This cloud is described mathematically by a wave function.

As bizarre as these concepts seem, they're supported by many experimental results and have been used to build much of the technology that powers our modern world. Quantum mechanics forms the basis of the laser, semiconductors, and magnetic resonance imaging (MRI), and in the future, it will likely form the basis of new industries, like quantum computing.

Quantum computing is a sexy, popular topic nowadays. It takes advantage of quantum bits, or qubits, which can exist in both states '0' and '1' at the same time, processing much more information than classical bits. It's one future-facing application of quantum mechanics, and like many others, it promises to change our world significantly.

However, despite its enormous success, quantum mechanics isn't without its share of controversies or interpretations. The most famous one perhaps being the "Copenhagen interpretation," which says that a quantum system remains in superposition until it interacts with or is observed by the external world.

XVI

Harnessing the Laws of Nature

The concept of Harnessing the Laws of Nature refers to humanity's ability to understand and manipulate the fundamental principles that govern the natural world, thereby utilising them for various purposes. By grasping the intricate workings of these laws, scientists and engineers can design innovative technologies and systems that enhance human life and advance our collective knowledge.

The Laws of Nature

The unparalleled complexity and pragmatism of nature, in both its majesty and cryptic guise, are perpetually stunning. Nature's ordinances articulate a beautiful symbiosis, a harmony where both chaos and order exist concomitantly, which is key to our existence. In our unending strides towards advancements, it is becoming essential to combine our knowledge with these laws, harnessing them optimally in various sectors, such as energy production, architecture, and agriculture, among others.

From antiquity, humans have sought understanding by observing nature, often emulating its workings. This approach, termed "biomimicry" or "biomimetics," is an aspiration to replicate nature's methods and elements to solve human problems. By exploring how nature can inspire us, we can harness its laws in various industries.

One of the prime examples is energy production. To ensure sustainability and mitigate climate change, we need to continually explore nature-friendly energy sources. Sunlight, wind, and geothermal energy are vast, inexhaustible sources that nature provides us. Solar panels convert sunlight into electricity, embodying principles similar to what happens during photosynthesis in plants. Wind turbines, another critical sustainable energy factory, mirror the workings of the physiology of many birds where they convert air movement into kinetic energy.

Harnessing nature's laws is also evident in architecture and engineering. By considering nature's dynamics, architects and engineers can develop resilient, sustainable designs. For instance, the Eastgate Centre in Harare, Zimbabwe, uses a ventilation system resembling termite mounds, a testament to biomimicry. The structure maintains a cool internal atmosphere without the need for air conditioning, thus reducing energy consumption.

Furthermore, agricultural practices that harness nature's laws can create sustainable food systems and secure our future food supply. Strides such as agroforestry, where trees and crops intermingle, mimic natural forest ecosystems, leading to more efficient use of water and nutrients, and enhanced carbon sequestration.

Nature's laws, however, are not only for energy, architecture, and food production. They also hold sway in other areas, such as waste management and recycling. Nature thrives on cycles, with nothing going to waste. The principle of using waste as a resource is becoming increasingly significant as societies deal with ever-growing amounts of waste.

By harnessing nature's laws, a sustainable, resilient future becomes tangible. Yet, understanding and applying these laws requires a profound cognitive shift. We must learn to see ourselves not as dominants or conquerors of nature, but as a part of it, interdependent and interconnected. This approach will not merely offer immediate benefits but also help ensure long-term survival.

Harnessing nature's laws also implies building upon our scientific understanding and technological acumen, guided by the compass of wisdom. Furthermore, it requires concerted effort from diverse stakeholders, including scientists, policy-makers, businesses, and communities, all working in synergy towards a common goal, a sustainable future.

XVII

Exploring the Possibilities of Quantum Computing

The present discourse aims to delve into the multifaceted realm of quantum computing, investigating its vast potential and the myriad possibilities it offers for revolutionising the field of computation. Quantum computing, as an emerging field at the intersection of physics and computer science, harnesses quantum mechanics principles to perform computations that transcend the limitations of classical computers.

What is Quantum Computing?

Quantum computing is a paradigm in computer science that harnesses the principles of quantum mechanics to revolutionise computation. Its underlying concept lies in utilising quantum bits, or qubits, which can exist in multiple states simultaneously due to the phenomena of superposition and entanglement. These qubits are not limited to binary values like classical bits; instead, they can be in a multitude of states simultaneously, leading to an exponentially larger information processing capacity.

By exploiting this inherent feature, quantum computers have the potential to solve computational problems that are currently beyond the reach of classical computers. Quantum algorithms aim to manipulate and control qubit states through operations such as quantum gates, thereby enabling complex calculations with remarkable efficiency. Furthermore, the ability of qubits to be entangled allows for correlation between remote particles instantaneously, facilitating parallelism and vastly accelerating computational speed.

However, it is essential to note that the field of quantum computing is still in its nascent stages due to numerous technological challenges. Achieving stable qubits with minimal error rates remains a significant challenge since environmental factors readily disrupt their delicate quantum states. Additionally, developing scalable hardware architectures capable of incorporating a large number of qubits while maintaining coherence poses substantial obstacles.

Quantum computing represents an exciting frontier within computer science that employs the principles of quantum mechanics to revolutionise computation. By leveraging the unique properties of qubits, such as superposition and entanglement, researchers anticipate exponential advancements in solving complex computational problems.

What Are the Different Types of Quantum Computers?

The realm of quantum computing encompasses a diverse array of computational paradigms, each exhibiting distinct characteristics and potential applications. Multiple types of quantum computers have been proposed and developed, showcasing their unique architectures and underlying principles. Here, we delve into a concise enumeration of the various types of quantum computers:

1. Universal Quantum Computers: These devices represent the pinnacle of quantum computation, capable of performing any arbitrary quantum calculation. Utilising qubits as their fundamental units of information, universal quantum computers possess enormous computational power but are particularly challenging to construct due to requirements for error correction.

2. Quantum Annealers: Focused on solving optimization problems, these machines utilise qubits to explore vast solution spaces and identify optimal configurations using techniques like simulated annealing or quantum annealing. Quantum annealers excel in tackling specific problem domains like combinatorial optimization or machine learning tasks that can be formulated as optimization problems.

3. Adiabatic Quantum Computers: Operating based on adiabatic evolution principles, these devices leverage

adiabatic transformations to solve complex calculations. By exploiting slowly changing Hamiltonians during computation, they mitigate certain errors associated with other forms of quantum computing.

4. Topological Quantum Computers: A promising avenue for fault-tolerant computation, topological quantum computers employ quasi-particles exhibiting exotic properties, as building blocks for performing operations. These robust systems protect against decoherence and noise by storing and manipulating information within topological states.

How Can Quantum Computing Be Used to Solve Complex Problems?

Harnessing the principles of quantum mechanics, these novel computational systems exploit quantum bits or qubits, which can exist in multiple states simultaneously. This property enables quantum computers to perform parallel computations and explore vast solution spaces more efficiently than classical counterparts.

1. Quantum Superposition: By leveraging the phenomenon of superposition, quantum computers can represent a multitude of possibilities simultaneously. This allows them to explore various combinations of inputs and evaluate multiple solutions concurrently, ultimately leading to faster problem-solving.

2. Quantum Entanglement: Another crucial concept in quantum computing is entanglement, wherein two or more qubits become linked together in a way that their states are dependent on each other. This correlation allows for instantaneous communication between entangled qubits regardless of distance, enhancing computational efficiency and enabling faster information processing.

3. Quantum Algorithms: Quantum computing also offers new algorithms specifically designed to solve complex problems efficiently. For instance, Shor's algorithm utilises the inherent properties of quantum systems to factor large numbers exponentially faster than classical algorithms.

Similarly, Grover's algorithm accelerates database searches by exploiting quantum parallelism and amplitude amplification techniques.

XVIII

Supercomputers and the Future of Computational Physics

The emerging era of supercomputers holds immense promise for the future of computational physics, with its potential to revolutionise our understanding of complex physical phenomena. These advanced computing systems, characterised by their superior processing power and parallel architecture, enable scientists to tackle computationally intensive problems that were previously infeasible.

Types of Supercomputers

Supercomputers, with their incredible speed and processing power, have revolutionised how data computation is conducted in fields such as advanced scientific simulations, explorations, complex mathematical calculations, and data-intensive computing tasks. These advanced computing systems come in different types, each possessing unique attributes and functionalities that cater to various computing needs and preferences.

1. Vector Supercomputers:

Vector supercomputers are a type of supercomputing architecture that employs vector processors to handle large data sets. They perform complex computational tasks by efficiently processing long data arrays instead of single data items. This characteristic renders them ideal for scientific computational tasks that require handling massive quantities of data in parallel.

For instance, weather forecasting, which receives massive amounts of data from different meteorological stations worldwide, makes optimal use of vector supercomputers due to their capabilities in dealing with large datasets. Similarly, fields such as aerodynamic simulations and particle physics also use vector supercomputers because of their need for high computational efficiency.

2. Cluster Supercomputers:

Cluster supercomputers comprise a multitude of minicomputers or workstations connected via a high-speed network, forming what is known as distributed memory architecture. Each independent system, or 'node,' operates on its data, sharing the results with others across the network. This arrangement promotes parallel processing and increases computational speed.

Cluster supercomputers are popular in academia and research owing to their ability for multi-tasking and optimal price-performance ratio. For example, search engine companies like Google and Bing use cluster computing to index the web and provide rapid search results.

3. Grid Supercomputers:

Grid supercomputers leverage networking technology, connecting geographically dispersed computers, and making them operate as a virtual supercomputer. This distributed computing model empowers resource sharing across networks, utilising idle processing power for multitasking.

This model is ideal for large scale research projects and simulations that require huge computing resources. SETI@home, a scientific project investigating extraterrestrial life, utilises grid computing to analyse radio signals from space.

4. Tightly-Coupled or MPP

Supercomputers:

Massively Parallel Processing (MPP) supercomputers, also known as tightly-coupled supercomputers, comprise multiple processors working synchronously on different parts of the same problem. These processors share a single memory space, optimally utilised for computation.

This architecture is used in applications demanding high computational accuracy and throughput like multi-dimensional simulations in climate modelling, fluid dynamics, and nuclear physics.

Advantages and Disadvantages of Supercomputers

There are certain associated pitfalls that cannot be ignored. Supercomputers are computational powerhouses. Their primary characteristic is their ability to perform multiple complex calculations simultaneously at tremendous speed. These machines process trillions of instructions per second, vastly surpassing the capability of regular computers.

The advantages supercomputers provide are myriad. Firstly, the scientific and medical research spheres benefit enormously from supercomputing in terms of simulation and modelling. Complex phenomena such as weather forecasting, nuclear reaction simulations, DNA decoding, or the creation of pharmaceutical drugs, significantly rely upon these powerful machines.

Furthermore, supercomputers, having near-impossible computational capabilities, lend their strengths to the finance sector. Institutions utilise supercomputers to analyse vast quantities of data, providing deep insight into market trends, risk management, and strategic decision-making.

Lastly, in the realm of national security and defence, supercomputers play a vital role. Military organisations employ supercomputers for strategy simulation, intelligence analysis, and advanced weaponry design.

Despite the plethora of supercomputers' advantages, several disadvantages ought to be considered. To start, their deployment can result in an immense energy footprint. Supercomputers require massive amounts of electricity to function, contributing to an unsustainable energy demand.

Secondly, the price of supercomputers is prohibitively high. Procurement, maintenance, and upgrading costs can run into billions of dollars, posing a significant financial barrier to many potential users.

A serious concern associated with supercomputers is security risk. Given these machines often work on confidential or classified data, breaches or cyber-attacks pose severe threats.

Lastly, the complexity of supercomputer operations and the need for advanced technical knowledge to operate such systems efficiently may limit its accessibility. This results in a steep learning curve and acts as a potential barrier to many prospective users.

To summarise, supercomputers stand as powerful allies in numerous sectors, providing vast processing capabilities that help researchers and analysts to solve complex problems. However, imperative aspects such as the high energy footprint, prohibitive costs, security concerns, and operational complexity render a sober examination of their use.

Given the pros and cons, it is apparent that while the benefits of supercomputers are numerous and significant, organisations must fully understand their potential drawbacks prior to implementation, only then, can the power of supercomputers be wielded effectively.

Applications of Supercomputers in Computational Physics

Utilisation in Climate Modeling

One of the core areas of computational physics where the application of supercomputers prevails is climate modelling. These models allow scientists to piece together the earth's climate complexities, forecasting future weather patterns and elements critical to environmental preservation. The massive computations required to process meteorological data from billions of grid points from around the world necessitate supercomputers, ensuring accurate predictions and providing valuable insight into climate and weather trends.

Quantum Physics and Quantum Computing

Quantum computing, the new frontier in technological advancement, heavily employs supercomputers to administer groundbreaking work in quantum physics. Equations integral to quantum mechanics research, such as Schrödinger's or Dirac's equations, can only be resolved through numerical methods that require enormous computational power. Supercomputers offer the unprecedented computational capability to handle colossal calculations and simulations integral to this field, granting scientists the power to decipher and predict quantum phenomena.

Astrophysics and Cosmology

Evidently, supercomputers' expansive processing capability has not left astrophysics and cosmology untouched. It's noteworthy how stellar evolutions, nebula dynamics, the formation of galaxies, and cosmological structures are now being simulated via supercomputers. Scientists can now dynamically model Black Hole collisions, predict galaxy formations and decipher Universe's expansion mysteries, often playing a crucial role in path-defining discoveries.

Nuclear Physics and Lattice Quantum Chromodynamics

Lattice Quantum Chromodynamics (QCD) allows researchers to numerically predict QCD phenomena, with supercomputers allowing the simulation of nuclear reactions and forces involved in atomic nuclei. Recent advancements in supercomputing have enabled physicists to achieve superior energy resolution and vastly improved spatial accuracy in modelling nuclear structures.

Material Sciences and Nanotechnology

Supercomputers are adding a critical dimension to material science and nanotechnology. They aid in the sophisticated examination of material properties at the atomic and molecular level, progressing work in the field of nanotechnology. The ability to model and simulate materials performance under various conditions aids in the development of new materials and enhancing existing ones.

XIX

Traditional Research Approaches Enabled by Computing

The concept of Traditional Research Approaches Enabled by Computing refers to the utilisation of computing technologies to enhance and facilitate conventional research methodologies across various academic disciplines. In contemporary academia, researchers harness the power of computing tools and techniques to streamline data collection, analysis, and interpretation processes.

Automated Text Analysis

Automated text analysis encompasses a range of methodologies that utilise computational tools to process large volumes of textual information systematically. This approach enables researchers to systematically examine various aspects of texts such as linguistic patterns, sentiment analysis, topic modelling, and named entity recognition. By automating these processes, researchers can efficiently analyse vast amounts of textual data that would otherwise be time-consuming or practically impossible for manual examination.

The application of automated text analysis techniques offers numerous advantages to traditional research approaches. Firstly, it allows for increased objectivity by minimising potential biases associated with human interpretation and judgement. Additionally, this approach enhances the scalability of research endeavours by enabling researchers to handle significantly larger datasets than previously feasible. Moreover, automated text analysis facilitates the identification and extraction of previously unnoticed patterns or relationships within texts, thereby offering novel insights into the subject matter under investigation. Overall, integrating computing technologies into traditional research paradigms through techniques like automated text analysis provides a valuable avenue for advancing knowledge across various academic disciplines.

One example illustrating the efficacy of automated text analysis is its application in sentiment analysis. By employing machine learning models and linguistic rule-based approaches, researchers can automatically assess the sentiment expressed in a vast number of online reviews or social media posts. This enables them to identify overall positive or negative sentiments towards specific products or services with remarkable accuracy.

Another notable application lies in topic modelling, which allows researchers to automatically discover latent topics or themes within a collection of documents. By leveraging algorithms such as Latent Dirichlet Allocation (LDA), they can uncover hidden patterns and gain deeper insights into complex phenomena across various fields like sociology, politics, or healthcare.

Predictive Analytics

Predictive analytics entails a multifaceted process that integrates various stages including data collection, preprocessing, feature selection, model building, and evaluation. Researchers harness advanced computational tools and algorithms to extract relevant information from complex datasets, identifying key variables that influence the outcome of interest. Through the use of modelling techniques such as regression analysis, decision trees, neural networks, or machine learning algorithms like random forests or support vector machines, researchers construct predictive models capable of making accurate forecasts based on historical observations.

By employing traditional research approaches enabled by computing such as predictive analytics, researchers are empowered to make informed decisions and anticipate future events. This methodology allows for the exploration of complex relationships between variables and uncovers hidden patterns within data. The integration of sophisticated computational techniques enables researchers to predict outcomes in fields ranging from finance and healthcare to marketing and environmental science. Overall, traditional research approaches leveraging computing capabilities are revolutionising research practices by providing novel avenues for analysis and prediction through the power of predictive analytics.

One illustrative example of predictive analytics lies in the field of finance. Through sophisticated data mining techniques, financial researchers can analyse historical market trends, economic indicators, and company-specific data to forecast stock prices and market movements. These predictions enable investors to make informed decisions regarding portfolio management, risk assessment, and asset allocation.

Another domain benefitting from predictive analytics is healthcare. Researchers leverage this approach to develop models that predict disease outbreaks or determine patients' susceptibility to certain conditions based on genetic predispositions and lifestyle factors. By identifying high-risk individuals or detecting early warning signs of diseases, healthcare practitioners can intervene proactively and allocate resources effectively, ultimately improving patient outcomes while reducing healthcare costs.

Qualitative and Quantitative Research

Traditional research approaches enabled by computing refer to the utilisation of computer technology in conducting qualitative and quantitative research. Qualitative research involves an exploratory investigation that aims to understand the underlying reasons, opinions, and motivations of individuals or groups, typically through interviews, observations, or analysis of textual data. By employing computing tools such as qualitative data analysis software (QDAS), researchers can efficiently manage large volumes of qualitative data, facilitate coding and categorization processes, and enhance the rigour and reliability of their findings.

The integration of computing in traditional research approaches provides several advantages:

1. Increased efficiency: Computing technologies enable researchers to process and analyse large datasets more quickly and accurately than manual methods.

2. Enhanced precision: By utilising advanced statistical software and algorithms, researchers can minimise human errors and obtain precise measurements.

3. Improved scalability: Computing allows for the collection of extensive data sets from diverse sources and facilitates the processing of complex analyses that would be otherwise impractical or time-consuming.

4. Expanded possibilities: The use of computing in traditional research approaches opens up new avenues for exploring phenomena that were previously challenging to investigate due to their complexity or scale.

XX

Challenges of Interdisciplinary Research

Interdisciplinary research, a scholarly pursuit characterised by the integration of knowledge and methodologies from multiple academic disciplines, presents a myriad of challenges that impede its successful execution.

Defining Interdisciplinary Research

A key characteristic of interdisciplinary research lies in its ability to transcend reductionist tendencies by embracing a systemic approach that acknowledges the interplay between multiple dimensions of knowledge production. It recognizes that complex phenomena cannot be fully comprehended through isolated disciplinary lenses but require an amalgamation of viewpoints and methods. Consequently, interdisciplinary research stimulates conceptual innovation by fostering dialectical interactions between divergent epistemologies, ontologies, and methodologies. Researchers engaged in this endeavour must navigate heterogeneous domains of knowledge while navigating the nuances and tensions inherent in integrating disparate disciplinary perspectives.

Furthermore, interdisciplinary research is characterised by its inclination towards transdisciplinarity, which extends beyond mere collaboration among disciplines to incorporate stakeholders beyond academia. By engaging various societal actors such as policymakers, practitioners, community members, or industry experts throughout the research process, it seeks to enhance the relevance and applicability of its findings for real-world challenges. This inclusiveness not only broadens the scope of inquiry but also fosters reciprocal learning between academia and society at large.

Identifying the Challenges of Interdisciplinary Research

In the realm of interdisciplinary research, scholars are confronted with an array of formidable challenges that demand keen attention and systematic investigation. These challenges can be summarised as follows:

1. Epistemological Incommensurability: The divergent epistemological frameworks employed in different disciplines often hinder coherent knowledge construction and integration across fields. This predicament arises due to disparate ontological assumptions, methodological approaches, and theoretical perspectives that impede meaningful dialogue and synthesis.

2. Disciplinary Boundaries: The rigid boundaries between disciplines pose a significant challenge to interdisciplinary research endeavours. These disciplinary siloes perpetuate insularity and hinder collaboration among researchers from various fields, preventing the exchange of ideas, methodologies, and insights necessary for holistic problem-solving.

3. Communication Gap: Effective communication is a cornerstone of interdisciplinary research but is frequently undermined by specialised jargon within individual disciplines. Unfamiliar terminology creates barriers to comprehension between researchers from different fields, inhibiting effective collaboration and knowledge transfer.

4. Methodological Complexities: Integrating diverse methodologies from multiple disciplines necessitates meticulous planning and coordination. Researchers must grapple with reconciling disparate data collection techniques, measurement instruments, and analytical frameworks to ensure the validity and reliability of findings generated through interdisciplinary collaboration.

5. Institutional Barriers: Academic institutions traditionally prioritise disciplinary-focused research over interdisciplinary endeavours, imposing structural constraints on researchers engaged in interdisciplinary pursuits.

Strategies for Successful Interdisciplinary Research

In the realm of academia, interdisciplinary research has become an increasingly prevalent and valued approach to tackle complex problems that require multifaceted perspectives. To ensure success in this endeavour, scholars must adopt several strategic approaches that foster collaboration and synergy across disciplines.

Key strategies for achieving successful interdisciplinary research include:

1. Foster a shared language: Establishing a common vocabulary and understanding among researchers from different fields is crucial for effective communication and knowledge exchange. This entails creating a space for open dialogue where disciplinary terminologies are clarified and translated, enabling seamless collaboration.

2. Encourage boundary-spanning expertise: Embrace diversity within interdisciplinary teams by assembling members with complementary skills and areas of expertise. By incorporating individuals from different backgrounds, such as scientists, artists, policymakers, or social scientists, a broader range of insights can be harnessed to address research questions more comprehensively.

3. Nurture strong leadership: Effective leadership plays a pivotal role in guiding interdisciplinary research endeavours towards productive outcomes. Leaders should possess

excellent communication skills, be adept at managing conflicts that may arise due to disciplinary differences, and foster an inclusive environment that values all contributions.

4. Promote interdisciplinary training: Encouraging educational programs that equip students with interdisciplinary skills is integral to cultivating future generations of successful researchers. Providing opportunities for cross-disciplinary training and collaborative projects enhances their ability to engage in meaningful interdisciplinary work throughout their careers.

XXI

252

Exploring the Intersection of Computing and Physics

The present scholarly discourse delves into a profound examination of the convergence of two intricate disciplines that have traditionally been perceived as distinct entities:computing and physics. This intellectual inquiry aims to unravel the multifaceted interplay between these domains, forging an understanding of the synergetic relationship that has emerged as a result of their integration.

Quantum Computing and Its Impact on Physics

Quantum computing, by virtue of its revolutionary technology, has emerged as one of the most interesting domains in the field of computational and theoretical physics. It is a branch of computation that applies the concepts of quantum mechanics to process information. Quantum computers, unlike classical computers that use 'bits' as their smallest unit of data, use 'qubits', short for 'quantum bits', which can leverage the principles of quantum mechanics to create exponentially greater computing power.

Underlying the realm of quantum computing are complex quantum mechanical phenomena like superposition and entanglement. The principle of superposition allows qubits to exist in multiple states simultaneously, thereby enabling quantum computers to work on multiple solutions at the same time. Entanglement, on the other hand, allows qubits that are in a superposition state to be correlated with each other, a change in one qubit could effectively cause changes in other correlated qubits, facilitating a rise in computational speed and power.

This quantum superposition and entanglement not only revolutionise the computing sector but might also lead to new paradigms in physics, giving fresh impetus to understand the laws governing the universe. Quantum computing, in essence, is acting as a simulator for quantum physics, enabling researchers to delve deeper into this area and understand several quantum phenomena.

- Physical Systems: Traditional computers struggle to accurately model the behaviour of particles at the quantum level due to their limited computational power. However, with quantum computers, scientists can potentially simulate and understand intricate phenomena such as chemical reactions or material properties on a whole new level.
- Research: Quantum computing could pave the way for advancements in fundamental physics research. For instance, researchers envision using quantum algorithms to analyse vast amounts of data collected from particle accelerators or astronomical observations more efficiently. This could lead to breakthroughs in fields like particle physics or astrophysics by uncovering hidden patterns and making connections that were previously impossible with classical computation.
- Simulation: With their extraordinary computational power, quantum computers can simulate complex systems at the molecular level with incredible accuracy. This opens up new possibilities for studying chemical reactions and understanding the behaviour of materials at an atomic scale.

Applying Machine Learning to Physical Phenomena

Physical phenomena encompass any naturally occurring events that can be observed and quantified. These could be anything from weather patterns, to seismic activities, to the motion of celestial bodies. The often complex and multidimensional nature of these phenomena make them ideal for the application of machine learning.

ML can be used to help predict these phenomena, understand them better and even find hidden patterns. ML models can be trained on historic and real-time data to predict outcomes or detect anomalies and patterns that could inform scientific theory or practice. For example, ML can be used to predict earthquake aftershocks or even predict the occurrence of extreme weather events such as tornadoes or hurricanes.

Code Example: Predicting Weather Patterns

Let's consider a basic implementation using Python and the Scikit-learn library for predicting weather patterns. Scikit-learn is a powerful and commonly used machine learning library in Python. For this demonstration, we will focus on predicting temperature.

(Note: This is a simple example and in a real-world application would require a more comprehensive approach and dataset)

```python
import pandas as pd

from sklearn.model_selection import import train_test_split

from sklearn.linear_model import LinearRegression

# loading dataset

df = pd.read_csv('weather.csv')

# select features and target

X = df[['humidity', 'pressure', 'wind_speed']]

y = df['temperature']

# splitting data

X_train, X_test, y_train, y_test = train_test_split(X, y, test_size=0.2, random_state=1)

# create model

model = LinearRegression()

# train model

model.fit(X_train, y_train)

# predict on test data
```

```
predictions = model.predict(X_test)
```

```

```

In this example, a simple linear regression model is used to predict temperature based on humidity, pressure, and wind_speed. The data is preprocessed, split into a training and test set (with 80% being used for training and 20% for testing), and finally, the model is trained and predictions are made.

The application of ML in studying physical phenomena brings a fresh perspective and new techniques into traditional scientific fields. Its predictive and analytical capabilities allow for more nuanced and in-depth studies. However, it is essential to remember that while ML is a powerful tool, it should complement, not replace, traditional scientific methods and critical thinking.

Using Artificial Intelligence to Improve Physics Experiments

The understanding of our natural world has been significantly advanced by physics. To further push the boundaries of this knowledge, scientists have begun to incorporate artificial intelligence (AI) into their experiments. AI's capacity to analyse large amounts of data quickly and accurately has been aptly deployed to improve the efficacy of physics experiments.

Artificial intelligence refers to the simulation of human intelligence processes by computer systems. Typically, these systems involve learning, reasoning, problem-solving, perception, and language understanding capabilities. The advent of AI has revolutionised all sectors of human endeavour, primarily science. Scientific experiments are becoming more complex, requiring more sophisticated tools for data analysis and interpretation; AI offers such sophistication.

One example of applying AI to physics experiments is in particle physics. In places like the Large Hadron Collider at CERN, where huge amounts of data are generated, AI is proving to be indispensable.

Traditionally, physicists would manually filter through petabytes of data looking for interesting events or anomalies. With AI, this information is processed automatically and much faster. For instance, a Machine-learning algorithm has been used to identify so-called 'jets' of particles that are created when high-energy protons collide.

```
# Python Code to identify particle 'jets'

from keras.models import Sequential

from keras.layers import Dense

# Define the model

model = Sequential()

model.add(Dense(units = 10, activation='relu', input_dim = 1000))

model.add(Dense(units = 1, activation='sigmoid'))

model.compile(loss='binary_crossentropy', optimizer='adam', metrics=['accuracy'])
```

This Python code demonstrates one way to create a simple AI model using the Keras library that could be trained to identify the 'jets'.

Quantum physics is another realm that has started profiting from AI. An example is the random search approach to 'quantum control problems'. Here, AI has been designed to find the optimal way to manipulate quantum systems without disturbing their delicate state.

Scientists have also developed a Machine-learning technique called 'Variance-Based Genetic Algorithm for Dimension Reduction' (VBGADR) to optimise physical simulations. This algorithm is efficient for reducing the dimensionality of a problem to improve computational efficiency, without significant loss of information.

```
```

```
# Sample code of VBGADR

def run_vbgadr():

learningrate = 0.2

num_population = 100

num_generations = 50

population = initialize_population(num_population)

for generation in range(num_generations):

population = evolve(population, learningrate)

run_vbgadr()
```

```
```

The example constitutes an outline for implementing the VBGADR algorithm in Particle Swarm Optimization problems.

The integration of AI into physics experiments is creating a paradigm shift in how data is analysed and interpreted.

The seamless interface between human intelligence and computational efficiency avails a promising future for Physics. However, the exploration of this technique must be pursued cautiously to avoid the pitfall of over-reliance, which could imperil the insightful role critical human thinking plays in scientific investigations.

Physics will continue to redefine humanity's understanding of the universe and natural phenomena. Nevertheless, as experimental systems grow bigger and more complex, AI tools are crucial to managing vast quantities of data to unearth new knowledge. AI aids data analysis and improves the precision and speed of experiments, thereby heralding the future of rigorous scientific investigations

Utilising Cloud Computing for Physics Research

Physics research often deals with enormous volumes of data that require substantial computational power for processing. This has necessitated the implementation of high-performance computing (HPC) infrastructures. However, such infrastructures are generally expensive to maintain, limiting their accessibility.

The advent of cloud computing has ushered in a new era of cost-effective, scalable, and highly accessible computing resources. An on-demand cloud environment provides researchers with unlimited access to computational tools, allowing them to perform complex calculations and simulations seamlessly.

The cloud also negates the need for investment in physical infrastructure and its associated maintenance costs, thus making advanced computing capabilities accessible to a broader spectrum of physics researchers. The facility to scale resources up and down as per demand ensures efficient utilisation of resources and mitigates the wastage of computational power.

Example of Cloud-Based Physics Research

The cloud's capacity for high-performance computations was put to the test when CERN (European Organization for Nuclear Research) utilised this technology for its Large Hadron Collider (LHC) project. The LHC, recognised as one of the most ambitious and complex projects in physics, required considerable data processing and storage capabilities. The cloud computing technology platform was found to be an able aide in providing the necessary computational infrastructure, coping with the enormous data volumes and providing cost-effective and scalable solutions.

Sample Code

Below is a simple example using Python to read data from a cloud storage, specifically Google Cloud Storage:

```
```

from google.cloud import storage

def download_blob(bucket_name, source_blob_name, destination_file_name):

"Accesses cloud storage, retrieves data and saves to specified local destination"

storage_client = storage.Client()

bucket = storage_client.bucket(bucket_name)

blob = bucket.blob(source_blob_name)

blob.download_to_filename(destination_file_name)

print("Download completed: {} downloaded to {}.".format(

```
source_blob_name,

destination_file_name))

download_blob('your-bucket','data/item.data', '/local/path/
item.data')

```

This Python script uses the Google Cloud Storage Library to read cloud-stored data and save it to a local file. It can be beneficial for researchers dealing with large volumes of physics data.

The advent and continual development of cloud computing have proven to be a boon for physics research, where handling enormous data volumes and running complex simulations are the norms. The potential for on-demand, scalable, and high-performance computing resources thus offers a promising platform for future advancements in physics research.

XXII

Designing Experiments Virtually

The concept of Designing Experiments Virtually refers to the process of planning and executing scientific experiments in a digital environment, primarily utilising computer simulations or virtual reality platforms. This approach has gained prominence in contemporary research due to its potential for cost-effectiveness, efficiency, and increased experimental control.

Overview of Virtual Experiments

The expanding field of science and technology in recent years has breathed new life into conventional learning methods and challenged the status quo of traditional education. One such innovation that has remarkably redefined science learning is through Virtual Experiments. This eminent trend of integrating technology with education has bridged the gap between theoretical and practical learning.

Virtual experiments are scientific experiments conducted in a digitally simulated environment. They are the brainchildren of e-learning that enable students to perform, analyse, and learn from a myriad of laboratory experiments in a safe and cost-effective manner. The integration of virtual experiments in the curriculum has a multitude of implications on the quality of education.

Firstly, it has broadened the reach of experiential learning in the field of science. Conventionally, laboratory-based experiments come with time constraints, equipment limitations, risk of hazardous substances, and chance of human error. In contrast, virtual experiments offer an interactive platform where the experiments can be repeated, paused, and analysed at any point in time.

Virtual experiments are also cost-effective and efficient. Students get to perform a plethora of complex laboratory experiments without the requirement of physical space, purchase of expensive equipment, and supply of consumables. Furthermore, these experiments can be conducted without any geographical constraints as they are readily available online.

Another significant advantage of virtual experiments is they provide a realistic and engaging learning atmosphere. These experiments are designed in such a way that it mirrors the real laboratory setting replicating the procedure, equipment, and even the slightest details so that students do not miss out on the real laboratory experience.

That being said, the role of a teacher becomes critical in the implementation of virtual experiments. Teachers need to guide students through the process and intervene when necessary to prevent the development of any misconceptions or ambiguous ideas. The aim is to strike a balance between virtual and traditional learning by amalgamating the best of both worlds.

The integration of virtual experiments in the education system is a progressive step towards revolutionising learning and teaching of the sciences. It has paved the way for hands-on experiential learning, overcoming the barriers of traditional practices. Virtual experiments have undoubtedly made science learning more accessible, realistic, efficient and engaging.

As the education sector continues to evolve digitally, the importance and relevance of virtual experiments are only set to increase. The future holds great potential for virtual experiments to become more immersive, using emerging technologies, such as virtual reality, augmented reality, and AI, to make learning more experiential and application-focused.

Tools for Designing Experiments Virtually

Experiment designing is essential in scientific studies as it helps to determine the relationship between variables. Thanks to the advances in technology, researchers now have the opportunity to design their experiments virtually. This approach saves them time, allows them to control factors and variables precisely, and reduces the overall costs of projects

Types of Tools for Designing Experiments Virtually

Some of the most commonly used tools for designing virtual experiments include Labster, ChemLab, and LabX. These platforms offer an in-depth virtual lab experience that allows students and researchers to visualise complex lab processes.

Labster is a virtual lab simulation tool that provides students with a safe and engaging lab learning experience. Similarly, ChemLab, a computer-based laboratory simulator, gives a realistic representation of a chemistry laboratory, providing students and educators a convenient platform for laboratory experiments. LabX, on the other hand, is specifically designed for physics experiments, offering a simulated environment for students to perform and analyse experiments.

Benefits of Virtual Experiment Designing Tools

Virtual experiment designing tools bring several benefits. Firstly, they provide a risk-free environment for researchers. By predicatively modelling the results in a virtual lab, researchers can avoid any potential risks associated with the experimental process.

Secondly, these tools save time and resources. By designing experiments virtually, scientists can significantly minimise the physical resources needed and the time required for the experiment. Virtual tools also allow for quick design changes to optimise the experimental process.

Thirdly, they boost experimental repeatability. Scientists can easily replicate their virtual design for future trials, facilitating data reproduction and resulting in higher confidence in study findings.

Challenges of Virtual Experiment Designing Tools

Despite the advantages, there are a few challenges with the use of virtual designing tools in experiments. One primary issue is the level of realism they offer compared to physical labs. While virtual tools have improved significantly, simulating a perfect replica of the lab environment is still a challenge.

Despite some limitations, virtual experiment designing tools have revolutionised the scientific study process. They have not only made the overall design of experiments streamlined but also facilitated efficient visualisation, ensuring researchers can conduct safe, effective, and repeatable experiments.

Tools

The first essential tool is MATLAB, a computing environment developed by MathWorks. It provides a platform for numerical computation and visualisation, lending itself particularly well to experimental design. MATLAB offers capabilities such as data analysis and visualisation, computational mathematics, and algorithm development. Its Simulink system models, simulates, and analyses dynamic systems, making it an excellent tool for experiment design.

R, a programming language and software environment for statistical computing and graphics, is another significant tool. It features a suite of operators for calculations on arrays and matrices, lists of data sets, statistical inference, and an extensive collection of intermediate tools for data analysis. It is extensible, allowing researchers to design bespoke tools for specific purposes.

Python is also a preferred tool for designing virtual experiments, with libraries such as NumPy for numerical computation, matplotlib for data visualisation, and SciPy for scientific computation. For machine learning experiments, libraries like scikit-learn and TensorFlow are highly useful.

NetLogo is another interactive, programmable modelling environment for simulating complex systems and designing experiments. It is ideal when experiments involve the behaviour of agents in a shared environment, such as in social or biological simulations.

For bioinformatics, Bioconductor stands as a robust open-source software for genomic data analysis and statistics, providing tools for experimental design and bioinformatics workflows.

Lastly, for designing experiments involving fluid dynamics, automotive, gas, and energy systems, the ANSYS Fluent stands out due to its advanced physics capabilities. It's an engineering design software that uses computational fluid dynamics for virtual prototyping and experimentation.

Common Mistakes to Avoid When Designing Experiments Virtually

As technological advancements continue to evolve, the education sector has witnessed a host of changes, including the way scientists design and conduct experiments. With virtual experimentation emerging as a popular tool in this digital era, it is essential for researchers to understand the common mistakes they need to avoid when designing experiments virtually.

Lack of Clear Objectives

One of the biggest mistakes often made in virtual experimentation is unclear objectives. Researchers must have a well-defined aim, with clear hypotheses that are testable and measurable. Without these, the experiment can become purposeless and difficult to control or measure. It is crucial to have a clear understanding of what the experiment seeks to investigate and how the results should be interpreted. Avoid this by carefully outlining your objectives before starting your experiment. Ensure that your experimental design directly addresses these objectives, and re-evaluate them as necessary, allowing your design to serve as an effective tool for scientific discovery.

Overcomplicating the Experiment

Designing a virtual experiment can be complex, especially because virtual environments allow for a level of flexibility and potential experimentation not possible in physical labs. However, researchers often make the mistake of overcomplicating their experiments, using advanced tools and techniques that may not be necessary for their objectives. Avoid excessive complexity by simplifying your experiment's design. Rather than integrating multiple complex features, focus on the essential elements necessary for achieving your objectives. Keep the experimental design simple, ensuring it stays within a manageable range of variables.

Not Considering Potential Sources of Error

Unlike physical experimentation, virtual experiments do not encounter the same types of errors due to environmental factors. However, there can still be sources of error in the data generated from the simulation. These can stem from the chosen methods, processing techniques, or other technical aspects. To prevent such errors, consider all potential sources at the designing stage. Take steps to minimise them, and ensure that any potential error sources are accounted for when interpreting results.

Ignoring the Importance of Replicability

Replicability is the capacity of an experiment to produce consistent results when performed under the same conditions. In virtual experiments, researchers should ensure they can reproduce experiments, which requires careful documentation of settings, procedures, and data. Prevent this mistake by accurately recording every aspect of your experiment. Use standardised software versions and meticulous methods that enhance the experiment's repeatability.

Over Reliance on Automation

While automation creates efficiency in virtual experimentation, relying too heavily on it may lead to oversight of unexpected anomalies or errors. Automated processes lack the nuanced human insight required to contextualise and interpret data correctly. To mitigate this, adopt a balanced approach. Combine automated processes with regular check-ins to monitor progress and results. Regular observation allows immediate response to any anomalies and facilitates the early identification of issues.

Disregarding Regular Checks and Data Quality Control

Maximum accuracy is crucial in scientific experiments. Despite the advanced capabilities of virtual experiments, one should not assume the data generated are always accurate. Overlooking quality control is a common mistake. Ensure high-quality data by incorporating regular checks. Confirm that the data align with your set parameters and expectations. Regular data scrutiny ensures consistency and allows you to catch anomalies promptly.

How to Ensure Quality Control When Designing Experiments Virtually?

Ensuring quality control when designing experiments virtually necessitates a meticulous adherence to methodological principles and an astute consideration of potential confounding factors. As the academic landscape increasingly incorporates remote methodologies, it becomes imperative to employ rigorous procedures to maintain the integrity and validity of scientific investigations. To accomplish this, researchers must meticulously define their research questions, articulate clearly stated hypotheses, and establish stringent criteria for participant selection.

Virtual experimentation demands vigilant attention to reliability and validity concerns. Researchers should guarantee that all necessary equipment and software are properly calibrated and functioning optimally. Rigorous monitoring of data collection processes is essential to identify any technical glitches or inconsistencies that may jeopardise the accuracy and credibility of results. Additionally, researchers must be attentive to potential biases introduced by the virtual environment, such as increased distractions or reduced participant engagement, which may influence experimental outcomes.

Maintaining open channels of communication among research collaborators is crucial for quality control in virtual experiments. Regular meetings should be organised to discuss ongoing issues, clarify protocols, address unexpected challenges, and ensure consistent implementation across all stages of the experiment. By adhering diligently to these established practices, researchers can significantly enhance the robustness and reliability of their virtual experiments, thereby upholding the standards expected in contemporary scientific investigations.

XXIII

Developing Algorithms to Model Physical Phenomena

The endeavour of developing algorithms to model physical phenomena encapsulates a multidimensional and intricate process rooted in the domain of computational science.

Definition of algorithms

An algorithm, within the realm of computer science, is commonly defined as a precise and well-defined set of instructions or rules that are followed to solve a specific problem. These instructions are typically formulated in a systematic and sequential manner, aiming to address a given task efficiently and reliably. In essence, algorithms serve as procedural recipes that guide the execution of computational tasks by breaking them down into smaller, more manageable steps.

Algorithms have a crucial role in computer science and related fields, facilitating the development of software systems and enabling efficient data processing. They provide a structured approach to problem-solving by defining clear inputs, expected outputs, and intermediate steps necessary to transform the former into the latter. Moreover, algorithms often incorporate control structures such as loops or conditional statements that govern the flow of execution based on various conditions or iterations.

The design and analysis of algorithms form an essential part of algorithmic theory, where researchers explore fundamental properties such as correctness, efficiency, scalability, and robustness. Various algorithmic paradigms exist across different domains; some commonly encountered ones include divide-and-conquer approaches, greedy strategies, dynamic programming techniques, or graph-based methodologies. By leveraging mathematical models and rigorous analysis methods such as time/space complexity analysis or asymptotic notation (e.g., Big O notation), researchers seek to understand the behaviour and performance characteristics of algorithms under different scenarios.

Tools and technologies used for developing algorithms to model physical phenomena

Among the most popular methodologies are computational physics and numerical simulation techniques, which essentially involve using computational resources to solve complex physical problems.

Fortran, one of the oldest high-level languages, is still widely used in scientific computing due to its computational efficiency. Many years of development have ensured Fortran has accumulated a vast amount of scientific libraries that computational physicists often find useful.

Python, a high-level, interpreted language known for its critical role in scientific computing, is used for the development of algorithms. Its popularity is driven by its scalability and flexibility, which makes it a fantastic choice to manipulate large data sets and perform complex mathematical operations. SciPy and NumPy are Python libraries that provide advanced mathematical functions and data structures to perform numerical computations.

Another critical tool is the MATLAB (Matrix Laboratory) programming environment, which allows implementation, testing, and visualisation of mathematical models on a relatively convenient, high-level platform.

However, tools for developing algorithms extend beyond programming languages. Software packages such as COMSOL Multiphysics, ANSYS, and Abaqus provide a platform for comprehensive simulations of engineering systems dominated by physical phenomena. These software packages offer graphical user interfaces for working with complicated physics-based mathematical models without writing any code, providing faster analysis and validation of your model.

Meanwhile, Wolfram Mathematica is an advanced computational tool used to develop algorithms to model physical phenomena. It provides a vast amount of built-in functionality, covering multiple areas like numerical and symbolic computation, visualisation, and algorithm development.

Another emerging technology is data analytics, powered by machine learning (ML) algorithms and artificial intelligence (AI). These tools can identify patterns and correlations within large, complex data sets, which could deliver valuable insights for physical phenomena modelling.

Recent years have seen great advances in quantum computing, a paradigm that could potentially revolutionise the computational capacity for modelling physical phenomena. Quantum algorithms, designed for quantum bits or qubits, leverage superposition and entanglement phenomena to achieve faster computations.

The benefits of these tools and technologies are vast, providing solutions to complex physical problems, enhancing our understanding of the universe, and offering innovation opportunities for industries such as aerospace, defence, and healthcare. As computational resources continue to advance, we look forward to the development of more sophisticated algorithms, providing deeper insight into our understanding of physical phenomena.

Potential applications of algorithms to model physical phenomena

The computational power of modern technology brings with itself immense possibilities. One particularly promising area involves the modelling of physical phenomena, made increasingly efficient by sophisticated algorithms. This groundbreaking technique has a broad range of applications that are capable of revolutionising a myriad of sectors.

One powerful application of these modelling algorithms is in predicting weather and climate patterns. Numerical weather prediction (NWP) uses mathematical models of the atmosphere and oceans alongside observational data to predict weather outcomes. This information holds considerable power for long-term strategic planning, particularly in areas prone to extreme weather conditions. Improved prediction abilities can result in more efficient evacuation strategies and consequently, a reduction in loss of life and property due to natural disasters.

Algorithms also play a crucial role in researching and understanding environmental changes and climate variations. They allow scientists to develop sophisticated models to simulate different climate scenarios, thereby facilitating the formulation of effective intervention strategies. These environmental models are valuable tools to counteract the threats we face due to global warming and climate change.

In the field of astronomy, many algorithms are being developed to process and interpret the large amounts of data obtained from telescopes, satellites and other observational tools. These allow researchers to identify patterns, detect anomalies, and develop more profound insights into the workings of our universe.

The field of fluid dynamics, which deals with how gases and liquids behave, also finds significant applications of algorithms in modelling physical phenomena. Sophisticated simulation models provide deep insights into biological fluid systems, thereby having substantial implications in the healthcare industry. These insights can be applied to study respiratory and cardiovascular systems in the human body to understand the physical principles underlying many diseases.

Algorithms also have potential applications in traffic and transport simulations. Autonomous vehicles and intelligent transportation systems can leverage the power of algorithms to simulate various scenarios, which can help in strategic planning and the design of efficient transportation systems. This not only reduces congestion but also improves public safety and overall economic efficiency.

In the world of finance, algorithms can be applied to model economic phenomena and financial markets. Quantitative algorithms can be used to model and predict market behaviour, which can lead to improved trading strategies and risk management techniques.

The versatile applications of algorithms in modelling physical phenomena extend even beyond these areas and continue to reshape how we interact with, and understand the world around us.

XXIV

Simulation of Complex Systems with Quantum Computing

The field of simulating complex systems with quantum computing is an emerging area of research that explores the potential of utilising quantum computing platforms to model and analyse intricate phenomena. Complex systems are characterised by a large number of interacting components, each with their own set of behaviours and relationships.

Techniques for Simulating Complex Systems with Quantum Computing

Quantum computing is an emerging field of study that utilises the principles of quantum mechanics to perform computations. This innovative technology holds significant promise in areas like cryptography, optimization, machine learning, and particularly the simulation of complex systems. Complex systems such as molecular systems, financial modelling, weather forecasting, and more, which traditionally require vast resources to simulate, can be significantly improved with quantum computing due to its inherent superiority in processing power and speed.

One crucial technique in quantum computing is Quantum Phase Estimation (QPE). It is a fundamental protocol in quantum algorithms that provides an estimate of the eigenvalue of a unitary operator. Effective use of QPE is vital in simulations involving complex systems such as quantum chemistry and physics. This algorithm forms the basis of many quantum simulation tasks and machinery, such as the Quantum Fourier Transform (QFT).

```python
# Python Pseudo-code for Quantum Phase Estimation

# Import necessary quantum computing libraries

from qiskit import QuantumCircuit, execute, Aer
```

```python
from qiskit.visualization import plot_histogram

# Initialize Quantum Circuit
qc = QuantumCircuit(4, 3)

qc.x(3)

for qubit in range(3):

qc.h(qubit)

repetitions = 1

for counting_qubit in range(3):

for _ in range(repetitions):

qc.cu1(math.pi/4, counting_qubit, 3);   # This is
controlled-U

repetitions *= 2

qc.swap(0, 2)

# Quantum Fourier Transform
for qubit in range(3):

qc.h(qubit)

for other_qubit in range(qubit):

qc.cu1(-math.pi/float(2**(qubit-other_qubit)),
other_qubit, qubit)
```

```
qc.h(qubit)
```

Another important technique involves quantum error correction. Errors are bound to happen in practical quantum computing settings due to the fragility of quantum states, especially during the simulation of large, complex systems. Quantum error correction codes (QECs) are tools designed to recognize and correct quantum errors. A classic example is the Surface Code, the leading error-correcting code that uses a two-dimensional lattice of qubits.

Quantum Annealing is also a significant simulation technique in quantum computing. The technique is used to find the global minimum of a given function over a given set of discrete candidate solutions. Quantum annealing exploits quantum mechanical properties like tunneling and entanglement to speed up the search process, making it especially useful while dealing with large, high-dimensional systems.

Lastly, the Variational Quantum Eigensolver (VQE) is a hybrid quantum-classical algorithm used to find the ground state energy of a molecule. It combines the quantum computer's power to efficiently manipulate and measure quantum states with classical optimization techniques to solve complex problems, making it ideal for simulating molecular systems.

```python
```

```
# Python Pseudo-code for Variational Quantum Eigensolver

# Import necessary quantum computing libraries

from qiskit.aqua.components.optimizers import COBYLA

from qiskit.aqua.algorithms import VQE

from qiskit.aqua.components.variational_forms import RYRZ

from qiskit import Aer

# Initialize Backend

backend = Aer.get_backend('statevector_simulator')

# Define optimizer and variational form

optimizer = COBYLA(maxiter=500)

var_form = RYRZ(num_qubits=4)

# Initialize VQE

vqe = VQE(operator=h2_matrix, var_form=var_form,
optimizer=optimizer)

# Run VQE

result = vqe.run(backend)

```
```

The above-mentioned techniques are intangible advancements in quantum computing that grant researchers
```

the power to simulate and understand complex systems like never before. However, these benefits are contingent upon further innovation and development in the field. Future research efforts should place strong emphasis on expanding the understanding of quantum physics and improving quantum technology, ensuring these techniques can be deployed efficiently and effectively.

Examples of Complex Systems Simulated with Quantum Computing

Quantum Computing stands at the forefront of a scientific revolution, promising to influence areas such as drug discovery, climate modelling, and financial risk management. These broad applications are possible thanks to the complex systems simulations they can perform, a task traditional computing fails at mastering perfectly.

Firstly, let's consider drug discovery. The conventional process of developing new drugs is often time-consuming and costly. However, quantum computing is beginning to change this narrative, particularly through the simulation of molecular structures. For instance, IBM's Quantum system has shown immense success in this practice, modelling both simple and complex chemical reactions with impressive accuracy. Similarly, the Vancouver-based company 1QBit has used quantum algorithms to assess potential treatments for diseases such as HIV and Leukaemia.

Then, there's the application in climate modelling. Predicting climate conditions and changes is a precarious task because of the multifaceted nature of the earth's climate system. Quantum computing could provide a solution, given its ability to simulate and predict complex climate systems more accurately. An excellent illustration of this is the partnership between D-Wave Systems and the Oak Ridge National Laboratory. The collaboration aims to use quantum technology to create more accurate climate predictions models.

In the realm of the financial industry, risk management is often a complex system. Quantum computing can help manage financial risks by allowing for the simulation of various market scenarios more quickly and accurately. QxBranch, a startup rooted in quantum computing technology, has simulated derivative portfolios' pricing structures by leveraging quantum algorithms. This kind of application could empower investors to make informed decisions and reduce risks.

Another notable mention is Quantum Computing Inc.'s QUBO solver being employed in traffic optimization in smart cities. While the realm of smart city planning is complex, requiring effective coordination of resources and systems, Quantum computing has emerged as a promising solution.

The modelling of complex systems, whether it's drug discovery, climate modelling, risk management in finance, or even traffic optimization in smart cities, is vastly becoming within reach, thanks to quantum computing. With innumerable potential applications, quantum computing is being hailed as the next powerful computing paradigm

XXV

Analysing Experimental Results with Computational Physics

The endeavour of scrutinising experimental outcomes through the framework of computational physics entails a multifaceted approach that combines various mathematical techniques, algorithms, and computational models. This methodological paradigm enables researchers to delve into the intricate details and underlying mechanisms governing physical phenomena, fostering a deeper understanding of observed experimental data.

Applying Computational Physics to Experimental Results

Computational physics is a domain that employs numerical analysis and algorithms to solve and define physical problems predominantly involving the manipulation and computational of large arrays of data; it is a branch of physics that deals with the numerical simulation of physical systems and physical phenomena.

As technological advancements continue to progress, physicist's ability to conduct experiments has significantly improved. However, the sheer complexity and volume of data produced by some experiments can prove hard to interpret without using computational physics, which provides a practical solution in such instances.

For instance, computational physics offers practical algorithms and computational tools that can help in analysing experimental data, useful in making sense of vast arrays of figures. It provides an invaluable avenue into reducing complexity by breaking down physical problems into a sequence of smaller, more straightforward operations. Therefore, it effectively bridges the gap between theory and experiment by providing a practical tool to understand the underlying physical processes.

When applied to experimental results, computational physics significantly decreases the time spent on data interpretation. It can streamline otherwise laborious tasks by leveraging high-speed computation and detailed analytics that a human operator might struggle to keep up with in real-time. More importantly, a computational physics model can do this while maintaining the same high level of accuracy.

A mathematician would selectively use the best mathematical models to replicate information from an experiment. However, limitations arise when these models can't replicate the granularity and complexities of real-life situations. Computational physics equations can yield more precise results using raw experimental data.

Moreover, models that rely on computational physics tools may also be adapted to represent variations in experimental conditions, thus providing a more accurate approach for understanding the changes in experimental outputs. These models can be adjusted to take into account outlier data, highlight trends and produce datasets with enough granularity to allow for accurate predictions.

One needs to recognize that learning computational physics involves knowledge in more than one discipline. It requires competencies in mathematics, physics, and computer programming; however, the pay-off is enormous as it allows the integration of a vast amount of experimental data into coherent, predictive models.

Analysing Experimental Results with Computational Physics

Python is widely renowned in the scientific community due to its simplicity and extensive library support. NumPy and SciPy libraries are most commonly used for numerical and scientific computing, providing robust functions for numerical interrogation. Matplotlib is a plotting library, often used to visualise data and experiment results.

As an example, let's imagine we have conducted a simple experiment: throwing a ball straight up in the air and analysing its motion. We have gathered some data (height versus time) and are attempting to extract the acceleration due to gravity.

Code:

```python
import numpy as np

import matplotlib.pyplot as plt

from scipy.optimize import curve_fit

# Our experimental data:

time_arr = np.array([0, 1, 2, 3, 4, 5]) # Time in seconds

height_arr = np.array([0, 25, 45, 65, 75, 90]) # Height in
metres
```

```
# Defining the theoretical motion equation:

def motion_equation(t, a, v0):

return 0.5 * a * t**2 + v0 * t

# Perform the curve fitting:

popt, pcov = curve_fit(motion_equation, time_arr, height_arr)

a, v0 = popt

# Visualising the experimental data and fitted curve:

plt.scatter(time_arr, height_arr, color='blue', label='Experimental data')

plt.plot(time_arr, motion_equation(time_arr, a, v0), color='red', label='Fitted curve')

plt.xlabel('Time (s)')

plt.ylabel('Height (m)')

plt.legend()

plt.show()

```
```

In the above example, we utilise the scipy.optimize.curve_fit function, which implements the least squares method to fit our theoretical model (motion equation) to the experimental data. The fitted parameters provide a measure
```

of the initial velocity ('v0') and the acceleration due to gravity ('a'). The Matplotlib library is then used to visualise the comparison between our experimental data and the fitted curve from our computational analysis.

XXVI

The Impact of Computing on Physics Research

The intersection of computing science and physics research has yielded profound ramifications for the domain of scientific inquiry. The advent of computational techniques has not only revolutionised data acquisition and analysis but has also advanced theoretical models, simulation methodologies, and prediction capabilities within the field of physics.

The role of computers in creating new knowledge in physics

The realm of physics research has been drastically transformed by the advent of computing technology. Innuendo, the use, and dependence on computers has not merely enhanced the efficiency and speed of research; it has also transformed the methodology, opening up new pathways for scientific exploration.

Traditionally, physics research was primarily experimental or theoretical. Experimental physics involves physical experiments and observations to gather data and confirm theories. Theoretical physics on the other hand, concerns the development of theories and models to explain physical phenomena. With the advent of computing, a third branch emerged: computational physics, often considered a hybrid of the two traditional fields.

Computational physics combines elements of both theory and experiment, using computers to simulate physical systems and solve complex equations more efficiently. Often, these systems are too complex to solve using traditional mathematical methods, or the experiments necessary to explore them are not feasible or ethical. This has led to a seismic shift in how physics research is conducted. The Large Hadron Collider's discovery of the Higgs Boson particle, a triumph of modern physics, was achieved through colossal amounts of data processing via computing techniques.

Moreover, computing has massively expanded the scope and scale of physics research. The ability to create detailed simulations and models has led to significant breakthroughs across multiple fields, from statistical mechanics to quantum physics. Particularly, it has revolutionised the field of cosmology, where simulations allow researchers to recreate the vast complexity of the universe and observe phenomena such as galaxy formation and evolution.

In addition, the data analysis capabilities that computing offers are invaluable. Large-scale projects such as the Sloan Digital Sky Survey, which seeks to map the universe in unprecedented detail, would be impossible without computing to process, analyse, and store the vast amount of data collected. Furthermore, advancements in machine learning and artificial intelligence algorithms are ushering in a new era of data-driven discovery in physics.

However, the increasing integration of computing into physics research also presents challenges. With the escalating complexity of simulations and data analysis tasks, there is a growing demand for computational literacy among physicists. Improving both computational skills and computing resources will be pivotal in maximising the impact of computing on physics research moving forward.

To start with, computers enhance data analysis in physics, an essential component of discovering new knowledge. Physicists are frequently faced with vast amounts of data to analyse, an undertaking virtually impossible without computational assistance. Furthermore, modern particle physics experiments, like those carried out at the Large Hadron Collider, generate data in the petabytes - a magnitude that necessitates sophisticated data handling and analysis. Computers allow physicists to not only handle this sheer volume but also tap into patterns, correlations, and trends that would otherwise remain obscured.

Secondly, computers play an integral part in modelling physical phenomena. Because of their immense speed and computational power, computers allow physicists to simulate complex scenarios that would be otherwise impractical or impossible to do in real-world experiments. Simulations replicate real-world situations digitally, which helps in predicting outcomes and exploring situations beyond experimental reach. Consequently, it makes the discovery of new knowledge feasible.

Beyond data analysis and modelling, computers are instrumental in theoretical physics. They certainly paved the way for novel approaches to computation-based theoretical physics, such as lattice quantum field theory. These computer-based techniques permit the exploration of realms that were previously unattainable by traditional mathematical methods, opening up swathes of new knowledge.

Finally, collaborative work, a cornerstone of modern physics research, is made more accessible by computers. They provide platforms for researchers worldwide to collaborate, share ideas, results, and hypotheses, thereby facilitating the creation of new knowledge. Case in point, the sharing of data collected from the Higgs boson project would have been impossible without computers and the internet.

How computers have enabled faster and more efficient data analysis

Computers have enabled faster data analysis predominantly through their ability to process massive volumes of data in minimal time. Traditionally, data analysis was a highly time-consuming endeavour that demanded significant manual effort. However, with the advent of computing technology, large data sets can be processed rapidly, with calculations and correlations made in the blink of an eye. This ability has democratised data analysis, making it more efficient and universally accessible.

Computers work in conjunction with data analysis software to facilitate this speedy processing. These software programs, which range from Excel to advanced software solutions such as Python, SPSS, and R, expedite the organisation, interpretation, and end presentation of collected data. Their ease of use, flexibility, and advanced capabilities are widely appreciated in academic, commercial, and governmental settings alike.

Moreover, computers have played a pivotal role in enabling the execution of complex data analysis. Techniques such as machine learning and artificial intelligence, which rely heavily on computational power, have come to the forefront of modern data analysis thanks to advanced computers. They excel in identifying patterns and generating insights from colossal volumes of structured and unstructured data in real-time. This real-time analysis ability has revolutionised multiple sectors, including finance, healthcare, and retail by enabling immediate strategic decision-making based on data-derived insights.

Additionally, contemporary computer systems boast redundancy and error-checking mechanisms that ensure data accuracy and consistency. These features minimise human error and increase data integrity, ensuring precise, reliable analysis results.

XXVII

Mitigating Inequality in Access to Quantum Computing

The discourse at hand revolves around the imperative task of ameliorating disparities in the realm of quantum computing accessibility. Quantum computing, as an emerging field, holds immense potential to revolutionize various sectors and advance scientific progress. However, it is crucial to acknowledge that the current landscape exhibits a significant discrepancy in access to quantum computing resources, thereby exacerbating societal inequalities.

Exploring the Root Causes of Inequality

In the realm of quantum computing, the crucial issue of mitigating inequality in access demands comprehensive examination to elucidate the underlying causes. This scholarly endeavour seeks to unravel the multifaceted factors contributing to disparities in quantum computing accessibility. The exploration delves into discerning the root causes through an intricate analysis of socioeconomic, geographic, and educational determinants that impede equitable participation in this cutting-edge field.

A profound understanding of the manifold inequalities necessitates a holistic examination encompassing economic disparities. Socioeconomic factors play a pivotal role in shaping access to quantum computing resources, as individuals from affluent backgrounds often possess superior financial means to procure necessary equipment and expertise. Moreover, geographic disparities exacerbate the existing inequality landscape by limiting physical proximity to quantum computing centres and research hubs. Unfavourable regional distribution perpetuates unequal access due to limited availability of infrastructure and networking opportunities.

Additionally, educational inequalities further compound the challenge of achieving parity in accessing quantum computing resources. Inequitable distribution of quality education at primary, secondary, and tertiary levels disproportionately affects underprivileged communities' ability to engage with this technology. Limited exposure to subjects such as mathematics, physics, and computer science hinders their capacity for meaningful participation in quantum computing endeavours.

To mitigate inequality effectively, it is imperative to identify these fundamental causes comprehensively and develop strategies that address each aspect systematically. Only through such an approach can we hope to dismantle barriers hindering equitable access to this transformative technological frontier.

Identifying Inequality in Quantum Computing

Inequality in the field of quantum computing can be apparent in multiple forms. The fear of a digital divide has amplified with the advent of advanced technologies like quantum computing. Geographic disparities, where research-intensive universities and companies located in technologically advanced regions have better access, contribute to the digital divide. Additionally, quantum computing, unlike classical computing, requires a high level of expertise, thus creating a gap between those who can understand and utilise these powerful tools and those who cannot.

Besides, economic disparities play a significant role. Quantum technology is an expensive field of research and development, thus eliminating individuals or institutions with limited funds from participation.

The Ramifications

The socio-technological inequality in the quantum computing field can facilitate a 'knowledge monopoly,' where only a handful of institutions or corporations can dictate the terms and conditions of this powerful technology. These institutions can disproportionately shape the world to their advantage, potentially perpetuating existing socio-economic inequalities.

Strategies to Mitigate Inequality in Quantum Computing

Promoting Education: By incorporating introductory courses on quantum computing and quantum physics in the general curriculum, we can ensure a wider understanding of the principles of the field. Digital platforms can provide free or inexpensive courses on quantum computing fundamentals.

Government Investment: Governments should invest in research and development of quantum computing, democratising its access. Implementing public-private partnerships can also ensure that technology does not remain the preserve of a select few corporations.

Expanding Infrastructure: Encouraging the expansion of quantum computing infrastructure to underprivileged areas can assist in mitigating geographic disparities. Quantum technologies should be deemed as public goods accessible to all.

XXVIII

Exploring Unconventional Applications

Quantum computing, a cutting-edge field in the realm of computer science, propels us into an era of computational power previously unimaginable. This paradigm shift is rooted in the principles of quantum mechanics, as it leverages the peculiar properties of quantum bits (qubits) to perform complex calculations at an exponentially faster rate than traditional computers.

What are the Limitations of Quantum Computing?

The realm of quantum computing, despite its immense potential, is not devoid of limitations. One primary limitation arises from the fragile nature of qubits, which are the fundamental units of information in a quantum computer.

These qubits are highly sensitive to external disturbances and can easily lose their quantum properties through a process known as decoherence. Consequently, maintaining the coherence and stability of qubits poses an ongoing challenge in quantum computing.

Moreover, another significant limitation lies in the complexity and scalability of quantum algorithms. Although quantum computers have shown promising performance on specific tasks like factorization and simulation, developing efficient algorithms that can be executed on a larger scale remains a formidable task. The inherent complexity arising from entanglement and superposition makes it difficult to design algorithms that outperform classical counterparts for general-purpose computing tasks.

Additionally, physical constraints present further limitations for practical implementations of quantum computers. The requirement for extreme cryogenic temperatures to minimise decoherence adds substantial overhead in terms of infrastructure and energy consumption. Furthermore, the need for precise control over individual qubits demands sophisticated error correction techniques to mitigate errors caused by various sources such as imperfect gates or interactions with the environment.

While quantum computing holds great promise for revolutionising computation in various fields due to its inherent parallelism and potential speedup over classical methods, limitations related to decoherence, algorithmic complexity, and physical constraints remain significant barriers that researchers must overcome to fully harness its power.

XXIX

Conclusion

Quantum computing stands as an innovative and promising paradigm that has the potential to revolutionise various fields of science and technology. Through harnessing the principles of quantum mechanics, this emerging discipline enables computational systems to manipulate information at the level of individual quantum states, known as qubits.

The Future of Quantum Computing

The field of quantum computing, which harnesses the peculiar laws of quantum mechanics, has been gathering momentum over the past few years. Quantum computing operates by leveraging the quantum states of subatomic particles to perform data operations. It promises exponentially greater processing power than conventional computers, offering the potential to revolutionise industries ranging from chemistry and materials science to machine learning and cryptography.

The future of quantum computing is increasingly becoming a topic of interest around the world today. Several tech giants, including Google, IBM, Microsoft, and China's Alibaba, have entered the quantum computing sphere, advancing research at a steady pace. This has made quantum supremacy or the point at which quantum computers outperform classic supercomputers, a reality.

One of the most promising aspects of quantum computing's future is in cryptography. Conventional cryptography systems rely on factorization problem-solving, a task that can be effortlessly cracked by quantum computers. This means quantum computing could potentially render current encryption techniques obsolete. In response to this potential threat, researchers are exploring quantum cryptography. Quantum key distribution (QKD) offers the unique feature of detecting any eavesdropping attempts, thus ensuring secure information transfer.

In the field of Material Science and Chemistry, quantum computers could aid in the simulation and understanding of complex molecules, a task which is currently impossible for any classic computer due to the quantum nature of molecules. This has vast implications for drug development and materials design in the coming decades.

Machine Learning and Artificial Intelligence are bound to be revolutionised with the arrival of quantum computing. Quantum machine learning, an emerging field, proposes to use quantum computers to speed up parts of the machine learning process. The acceleration of complex computations can vastly improve algorithms' efficiency and, thus, significantly impact in fields like data analysis, pattern recognition, and decision making.

Despite the vast potential of quantum computing, the realisation of a fully functional and reliable quantum computer still faces significant hurdles. Issues pertaining to qubit stability, error correction, and the need for ultra-low temperature environments are ongoing challenges.

Nonetheless, the venture capital investments in quantum technology startups have shown exponential growth signifying expectant advancements. Furthermore, to equip the future generation with quantum literacy, educational initiatives like "quantum in the classroom," where students receive hands-on experience with quantum computing, are taking cognizance.

Quantum computing is invariably the next frontier in computer science. Its implications are far-reaching and profound. Although the technology is still in its infancy, with much left to explore and optimise, its anticipated arrival is already beginning to shape industries in their methodological approach.

As we plan for this future, it's vital to create meaningful dialogue and policy-making in step with this impending technological leap, ensuring societal understanding of the applications and ethical implications of quantum computing. The future is here, and it's quantum.

Conclusion

Quantum computing is a complex and compelling field of study that continues to extend the boundaries of our understanding in computer science and physics. With an optimistic view, one can say that the potential of quantum computing to offer solutions and redesign systems that shape our world is vast and revolutionary. From its potential to solve complex mathematical problems to running various simulations or enhancing encryption, it clearly indicates that a new era in computing capabilities is steadily approaching.

The impact of quantum computing would not only be limited to just the technology sector. It would call upon a fundamental shift across several fields such as healthcare, logistics, artificial intelligence, cryptography, and financial services. In fact, numerous global entities like IBM, Google, and Microsoft are investing billions in the pursuit of developing scalable quantum computers.

Quantum computing operates on the principle of quantum mechanics, where qubits, the quantum equivalent of classical bits are utilised. The key differentiator is that while classical bits can exist in one state at a time, either a 0 or a 1, qubits can exist in both states at once. This property enables quantum computers to perform calculations at a speed and capacity presently unattainable by their classical counterparts.

Encryption, due to its complex nature, can significantly benefit from quantum computing. Traditional cryptographic keys that now take an astronomical amount of computational effort to crack could be computed swiftly using quantum computers. For this reason, organisations worldwide have already been incorporating quantum-resistant algorithms into their security protocols.

Another promising application of quantum computing is drug discovery, where a quantum computer's superposition feature could compute and analyse molecular data at exceptional speeds, resulting in fast-track discoveries. Similarly, in finance, quantum computing's ability to process vast quantities of data simultaneously could expedite risk management, trading strategies, or financial modelling, offering a competitive advantage to businesses.

Despite these exciting prospects, it should be remembered that quantum computing is still in nascent stages, facing a host of technical challenges. Issues of quantum coherence, error correction, and creating scalable quantum computers are yet to be fully surmounted. But with emerging technologies such as topological quantum computing and Quantum annealing, these problems aren't insurmountable.

As humanity gradually moves past classical computing limitations, the quantum computing era will inevitably dawn, ushering us into a future full of unprecedented possibilities. However, it's crucial that as we navigate into this technological evolution, we do so with an understanding of potential ethical implications and risks, thus ensuring a safe digital world for everyone.

Don't miss out!

Visit the website below and you can sign up to receive emails whenever Lab Maharaj publishes a new book. There's no charge and no obligation.

https://books2read.com/r/B-A-ZAZX-YPPMC

BOOKS2READ

Connecting independent readers to independent writers.

Did you love *Quantum Quandaries*? Then you should read *Artificial Intelligence and the Future of Humanity*[1] by Lab Maharaj!

[2]

In Artificial Intelligence and the Future of Humanity, we explore the ethical, economic, and political implications of this technology. The book examines the potential of AI to create a more equitable and just world, as well as the potential pitfalls of allowing machines to take over human labor. It also provides an overview of the current state of AI and how it has developed over the years, and provides an outlook on its potential future applications.

---

1. https://books2read.com/u/b5WK2G

2. https://books2read.com/u/b5WK2G

This book is a must-read for anyone who is interested in understanding the impacts of AI on our society and the future of humanity. It is an insightful and thought-provoking exploration of the potential implications of artificial intelligence and its potential to shape our world. Read more at https://www.labmaharaj.com.

Also by Lab Maharaj

Unshakeable Fellowship: A Journey to Deepen Your
Connection with God
The Philosopher's Journey: A History of Thought
The Digital Marketing Handbook: A Comprehensive
Guide to Online Advertising
Artificial Intelligence and the Future of Humanity
The Path of Stoics
Quantum Quandaries

Watch for more at https://www.labmaharaj.com.

About the Author

Lab Maharaj is an ambitious and creative student currently pursuing a Doctor of Computer Science degree, specializing in Artificial Intelligence and Machine Learning. With a passion for learning, Lab has a diverse set of interests that span across multiple disciplines, including Computers, Physics, Mathematics, Languages, Visual Arts, Baking, and Video Games. She has a Master's degree in Information Systems and Cybersecurity and has conducted research in the areas of Deep Learning, Natural Language Processing and Knowledge Representation. With a broad knowledge of programming languages like Python, Java and C++, she is well-equipped to develop modern Artificial Intelligence applications.

Lab Maharaj is also an author who has written books on philosophy, digital marketing and artificial intelligence. Her passion for learning and her drive to explore new ideas and concepts make her a valuable asset to the AI field. She is also an inspiring role model for young learners and a dedicated advocate for the advancement of AI technology.

Read more at https://www.labmaharaj.com.

www.ingramcontent.com/pod-product-compliance
Lightning Source LLC
Chambersburg PA
CBHW061503120726

48001CB00004B/1192